GARDENS *of* FRANCE

GARDENS *of* FRANCE

PATRICK TAYLOR

MITCHELL BEAZLEY

A ma mère
"Heureux qui, comme Ulysse, a fait un beau voyage"

First published in 1998 by Mitchell Beazley, an imprint of
Reed Consumer Books Limited, London
London SW3 6RB
and Auckland, Melbourne, Singapore and Toronto

ISBN 1 85732 873 6

Executive Art Editor: Ruth Hope
Executive Editor: Guy Croton
Designer: Terry Hirst
Editor: Selina Mumford
Editorial Assistant: Anna Nicholas
Production: Rachel Staveley
Illustrator: Kevin Robinson
Cartographer: Kevin Jones
Picture Researcher: Anna Kobryn

Half title: Palais de la Berbie;
Title: Château de Chenonceau;
Contents: Château de Canon

The publisher wishes to thank all those who contributed in
collating reference material for the feature gardens.

Printed in Singapore

Contents

How to use this book

This guide is intended for travellers who wish to visit the most historic and beautiful gardens of France. The book is divided into five chapters covering five major regions of France. Each chapter comprises an introductory section with a regional map and a list of the gardens, followed by entries on each garden. The entries are accompanied by detailed at-a-glance information telling the reader about the garden's defining characteristics and nearby sights of interest. The guide also includes five "feature" gardens, specially illustrated by three-dimensional plans.

List of gardens

Map showing tours, gardens and general location

Key to roads, towns and garden tours

Photographs of special features

Plan of the garden

Garden number relates to tour map at the beginning of the chapter

Garden opening times

House opening times

Address and/or telephone number for information

Sights of interest within easy travelling distance

Garden name

Location of garden

Information about garden

KEY

- 🖢 Admission charge
- 🍽 Refreshments in nearby vicinity
- ❖ Formal garden
- ⚞ Landscape garden
- ⚶ House major feature
- ⊞ Historic garden
- ⫲ Kitchen garden
- ⚘ Botanic interest/rare plants
- ⚵ Topiary
- ≋ Borders
- ⛲ Water features
- ⚱ Architectural/ornamental features

Foreword

It is a myth that all French gardens are of rigid formality, filled with topiary and tortured trees. No doubt the formal gardens of the 17th century, of which Versailles is the model, strike a deep note in the French character. But the French character, as anyone who has been to France knows perfectly well, is richly complex, not to be explained by a handful of clichés. In the Introduction to this book I emphasize the two great French traditions of the Baroque garden and the municipal garden. But that is like saying the best wines in France are claret and burgandy – a horribly inadequate partial truth. For in gardening, as in viticulture, France has a wonderful diverse and vigorous tradition. In my choice of gardens for this book I have tried to reflect this diversity. No country on earth can show such a range of gardens as the modernist Villa Noailles, the historic arboretum of Chèvreloup, the *potager* at Villandry, the futuristic Parc de la Villette, and the fastidious plantsmanship of Kerdalo.

The early 20th-century rose garden at Bagatelle in the Bois de Boulogne.

Introduction

My French grandmother introduced me to French gardens, taking me as a child to the Champs de Juillet in Limoges in 1946. Since then I have seen gardens, public and private, all over the country. From April to September 1996 I made repeated sorties, revisiting old favourites, making new discoveries and immersing myself in the world of gardens. In this book I have made a personal selection, and although I have included one or two charming eccentricities (like the unforgettable Maison Picassiette in Chartres (see p.58), which some would scarcely regard as a garden at all) I do not think I have omitted any of the arguably great gardens.

Gardens of the quality of Versailles (see pp.80–3) or Vaux-le-Vicomte (see p.79), apart from being essential to an understanding of the development of French gardens, are marvellous places to visit. But I also hope to convey the full range of gardens in France. The Jardin Dumaine at Luçon (see p.117) in the Vendée, with its exquisite topiary figures and flawless *mosaïculture* teetering on the edge of kitsch, is just as much a part of the tradition of French gardening as the giant landscapes of André le Nôtre.

The two most distinctive types of garden are, I believe, 17th-century Baroque gardens and their later derivatives, and the public gardens. The latter exist in a staggering range of styles, from the Jardin de la Fontaine in Nîmes (see p.134) – 18th century but with Roman origins – to the sparkling new Parc André Citroën in Paris (see pp.94–5). No country in the world can show anything to compare with them.

At the Bois des Moutiers in Normandy, a Lutyens house with a Jekyll garden are given a fine French flavour.

I make no attempt to grade gardens in order of excellence – a futile exercise. But I hope by the warmth of my descriptions it is plain which are closest to my heart. I have included some gardens, almost always privately owned, which are not well maintained. But I have chosen them because they have powerful historic character or because of the charm of their romantic dishevelment.

Climate, geography and history are the key influences that determine a country's gardens. France has an amazing diversity of climates: the balmy Mediterranean, the snow-capped mountains and high meadows of the Haute-Alpes, and the high rainfall and mild climate of the coasts of Brittany and Normandy. France has about 4,000 species of native flowering plants but the diverse climates allow the cultivation of tens of thousands of exotics introduced from all over the world.

Geography made France one of the great seafaring countries, with major ports on the Mediterranean, the Atlantic and the Channel – new plants brought by sailors and merchants flooded in. Louis XV in 1726 issued a command that all "Captains of ships in Nantes should bring back seeds and plants from the overseas colonies."

Diana, the huntress at the Château de Champs – a brilliant recreation of a 17th-century garden.

The serene 17th-century Château de Courson overlooks a park of fine trees dispersed about a lake.

From the French colony in North America many new plants were introduced in the 17th century. The exploits of Père David and the Abbé Delavay in the 19th century introduced marvellous new plants from China. Dynasties of nurserymen – René Morin in the 17th century and the Vilmorin family from the 18th century onwards – brought countless new plants into commerce.

In the Middle Ages monastic communities gave a great impetus to the practice of horticulture and the study of plants. At the Abbaye Royale de Fontevraud (see p.25) one may see recreated Medieval gardens which vividly show the garden riches of France at that time. The Italian connection, with the marriage of Henri II to Catherine de'Medici in 1533, proved a decisive influence. As a result France was the first country outside Italy to put into practice the new ideas in architecture and garden design. This Renaissance harmony and discipline lay at the heart of le Nôtre's designs in the following century. In the 18th century English landscaping ideas exerted a powerful influence, resulting in masterpieces such as the Parc Jean-Jacques Rousseau (see p.75) but also, alas, sweeping away countless earlier formal gardens. Some of these were returned to their 17th-century appearance by the remarkable work of Henri and Achille Duchêne, father and son, in the later 19th and early 20th century.

In the 19th century, with the explosion of urban development, the public park flourished all over France. Not only have many 19th-century parks been impeccably restored but new parks have been created, such as the Parc de la Villette in Paris (see p.101). While the *jardin à la française* may rightly be thought of as the characteristic expression of the French genius for gardening, it is a myth that it is the only kind of garden found in France. Every type of garden is found and for garden visitors will provide experiences to be enjoyed nowhere else.

The pergola at Le Bois des Moutiers links the enclosures to the south of the house.

Key to gardens

1 Château d'Angers
2 Parc Floral d'Apremont
3 Château de Balleroy
4 Bourges: Jardin de l'Archevêché
5 Bourges: Jardin des Prés-Fichaux
6 Château de Brécy
7 Caen: Jardin des Plantes
8 Château de Canon
9 Château de Caradeuc
10 Château de Chenonceau
11 Cherbourg: Parc Emmanuel Liais
12 Jardin Public de Coutances
13 Dunkerque: Jardin du Musée d'Art Contemporain
14 Abbaye Royale de Fontevraud
15 Kerdalo
16 Château de Langeais
17 Parc Oriental de Maulévrier
18 Château de Miromesnil
19 Mont-Saint-Michel: Jardin du Cloître
20 Le Bois des Moutiers
21 Nantes: Parc de la Beaujoire
22 Nantes: Jardin des Plantes
23 Orléans: Parc Floral de la Source
24 Les Jardins du Prieuré Notre Dame d'Orsan
25 Château du Pin
26 Jardins de Plantbessin
27 Rennes: Parc du Thabor
28 Parc de Richelieu
29 Château de Sassy
30 Thury-Harcourt: Château d'Harcourt
31 Tours: Jardin Botanique
32 Château d'Ussé
33 Le Vasterival
34 Vernon: Château de Bizy
35 Château de Villandry

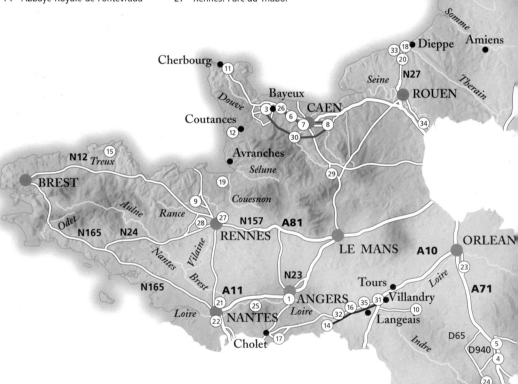

Key

═══ Motorways
─── Principal trunk highways
③ Gardens
● Major towns and cities
• Towns

Garden tours

▬▬ Southern tour 14, 32, 16, 35, 31
▬▬ Northern tour: 26, 6, 7, 8, 30, 3

Northern France

Along the coasts of Brittany and Normandy the climate is a vital factor in garden-making. Favourable micro-climates close to the sea allow the cultivation of tender plants – but this is a different world from that of the Côte d'Azur. The rainfall is high on the northern coast, so this is not cactus country but it is, emphatically, a wonderful climate for growing the aristocratic Asian flowering shrubs which transformed garden taste in the 19th century: camellias, magnolias and rhododendrons. All these thrive in such gardens as Kerdalo (see p.26) on the Brittany coast, and Le Vasterival (see p.44) and Le Bois des Moutiers (see pp.30–33) in Normandy. The wind is the enemy of coastal gardens and the successful ones enjoy the protection of a valley site or of woodland – often both. A garden which spurns such protection, however, is that of the Musée d'Art Contemporain (see p.24) at Dunkerque, which makes a virtue of using native coastal plants growing in sand.

The area is rich in public gardens – few towns are without their *jardin des plantes*. Some of these are of exceptional quality – such as that at Nantes (see p.35)

At Apremont an elegant painted bridge brings an oriental note to the richly planted garden.

which is also superlatively maintained. Others show a quirkiness which I find particularly attractive. The Jardin des Plantes at Coutances (see p.24) has a layout of sprightly formality in which cartoon characters are picked out in bedding plants.

The secret countryside of Normandy, with its wooded valleys and rich land, has a tradition of gentlemanly provincial gardening which has produced gardens of rare character, many of which are still privately owned. The Château de Canon near Caen (see p.21) mixes some of the ingredients of English landscape gardening with French decorative panache. The Château de Brécy (see p.19) flaunts a formal terraced garden of heart-stopping beauty. By the River Orne, south of Caen, the gardens of the Château d'Harcourt (see p.41) make a special virtue of delicious walks along the river banks. A little further south, the Château de Sassy (see p.41) has a virtuoso *jardin à la française* jutting out below the castle walls.

In the Loire Valley the rich alluvial soil has provided agricultural wealth for many hundreds of years. Monastic communities were drawn to this region, of which a survivor is the Abbaye Royale de Fontevraud (see p.25). Gardens displaying plants grown in the Middle Ages add enormously to its interest. Great houses sprang up about the banks of the Loire, and the area boasts some of the finest, and most irresistibly attractive, architecture in all France. Who can resist the Château de Chenonceau (see pp.22–23), its arches of pale stone spanning the waters of the River Cher? The Loire Valley has long been famous for its kitchen gardening and in the parterres of the Château de Villandry (see pp.46–49) it is elevated to a high art. A journey from, say, Orléans to Saint Nazaire on the coast of southern Brittany where the Loire rushes out into the Atlantic offers exquisite landscape, great houses and gardens.

The Renaissance château at Villandry with its 20th-century formal period-style *potager*.

Château d'Angers

Location: In the centre of the town

▮ ▮◐ ▮ ▮▮ ▮

🏠 **Open:** Mar to Palm Sunday, daily, 9.30am–12.30pm, 2–6pm; Palm Sunday to May, daily, 9.30am–12.30pm, 2–6.30pm; Jun to 15 Sep, daily, 9.30am–12.30pm, 2–6.30pm; 16 Sep to Oct, daily, 9.30am–12.30pm, 2–6pm; Nov to Feb, daily, 9.30am–12.30pm, 2–5.30pm

🏛 **Open:** As above

Further information from:
2 promenade du Bout du Monde
Tel: 02 41 86 81 94
Fax: 02 41 87 17 50

Nearby sights of interest:
Angers (old town); Saumur (château, Musée des Arts Décoratifs).

A flowery parterre high up on the walls makes a pretty contrast with the castle ramparts.

The giant, 13th-century castle, with its immense pairs of corner towers, rears up in the centre of the city on the banks of the River Maine. It was built by Saint Louis (King Louis IX), who was inspired by memories of the crusader castles he had seen while he was in the Holy Land for the Seventh Crusade, between 1248 and 1254.

There are gardens of a municipal flavour in the waterless moat, lawns, and virtuoso displays of summer bedding schemes. Box topiary and hedges form the framework for fan-shaped beds of brilliant colours. These may be admired from outside the castle, without paying the entrance fee. But it is within the castle walls that the chief garden interest lies. In the main courtyard – whose walls are garlanded with climbing plants – a monumental parterre is fashioned of six squares of turf edged with deep box hedges. Each has a huge elongated crown fashioned of clipped yew at its centre. The prettiest garden, however, is hidden away, high up on the rampart walk where light-hearted and beautifully designed ornamental planting contrasts delightfully with the stern walls of the castle. Here a floriferous parterre with gravel walks and low hedges of santolina and box has clouds of white *Gaura lindheimeri*, blue *Ceratostigma plumbaginoides*, and pale pink *Lavatera* 'Barnsley'. Other borders have grey-leaved *Perovskia atriplicifolia*, its powder-blue flowers admirably associated with pale lemon-yellow lilies. A rectangular box-edged bed has square blocks of *Artemisia* 'Powis Castle', catmint, and rue, all edged with box. Small ornamental trees give shade – a row of medlars, and a beautiful *Koelreuteria paniculata* clinging to the very corner of the ramparts.

Alongside, on the site of the former king's vineyard, are a few newly planted grapevines. If wine is ever made at the Château d'Angers, it will be one of the world's most exclusive.

Parc Floral d'Apremont

Location: 56km (38 miles) SE of Bourges, in the centre of the village

The Parc Floral was made by Gilles de Brissac from 1971 and is one of the finest flower gardens in France. A feast of decorative planting is disposed about a pretty stone and tiled house. At the entrance, a herbaceous border is backed by a monumental hedge of hornbeam clipped into broad buttresses, each surmounted by a sphere. Against the hedge, peonies, oriental poppies, tall foxtail lilies (*Eremurus* species), delicate *Thalictrum flavum glaucum*, alstroemerias, and yellow daylilies make a lively display. Pink foxtail lilies rise up among blood-red peonies and there is a profusion of alliums, cranesbills, peonies, roses, sweet williams, and glaucous-leaved *Baptisia australis*. Up above, a sloping lawn on one side is studded with ornamental trees, and a deep curving border is planted with substantial shrubs. Nearby is the sound of rushing water where a cascade tumbles down into a lake. The oriental flavour of a bridge of Chinese inspiration is emphasized with junipers "poodled" in Japanese style, and shapely rocks disposed about the banks of the lake.

On the way back to the entrance there is another finely planted border. Below a hedge of hornbeam clipped into soaring pointed crenellations like slender pyramids is an arrangement of white-flowered plants – crinums, geraniums, peonies, and roses.

Open: Palm Sunday to last Sun in Sep, daily, 10am to 12 noon, 2–7pm
Open: Same dates as above, daily, 2–6pm (Sun, 2–5pm)

Further information from:
Apremont-sur-Allier,
18150 La-Guerche-sur-l'Aubois
Tel: 02 48 80 41 41
Fax: 02 48 80 45 17

Nearby sights of interest:
Cathédrale de Saint-Etienne.

The airy red and green bridge of Chinese inspiration.

 # Château de Balleroy

Location: 16km (10 miles) SW of Bayeux, in the centre of the village

The château was built between 1616 and 1636 by François Mansart in the characteristically elegant style of the French Renaissance. It was one of the theories of Renaissance garden design that house and garden should be threaded together on the same axis. Here the idea is taken further by linking the house and garden to the landscape beyond. At Balleroy the main street of the village to the east of the château forms an axial avenue running straight towards the house. The road is lined with pollarded silver limes (*Tilia tomentosa*) and its rise and fall conceals the château so that it is suddenly revealed in the distance.

Following the axis into the cour d'honneur of the château we find a pair of parterres de broderie. Swirling patterns of clipped box rise from a background of silver-grey gravel, with contrasting red-brown gravel at the centre and in the narrow beds that frame the parterres. There are no flowers here and the elegance of the austere patterns of box makes a perfect foil for the house.

Open: 2 May to 15 Oct, daily, 9am to 12 noon, 2–6pm
Open: As above

Further information from:
4490 Balleroy
Tel: 02 31 21 60 61
Fax: 02 31 21 51 77

Nearby sights of interest:
Bayeux (Tapisserie de la Reine Mathilde); Caen (Abbaye aux Hommes); sites of World War II Normandy landings.

Open: All year, daily, 8am to sunset

Further information from:
place Etienne-Dolet,
18000 Bourges
Tel: 02 48 57 80 00

Nearby sights of interest:
Cathédrale de Saint-Etienne; the
city of Bourges.

4 *Bourges: Jardin de l'Archevêché*

(Also known as Le Jardin de l'Hôtel de Ville)
Location: In the centre of Bourges, next to the cathedral

The 12th-century cathedral of Saint-Etienne, with its exquisite medieval stained glass, is one of the architectural glories of France. Immediately to the south-east of the apse is the Jardin de l'Archevêché spread out under the windows of the 17th-century Hôtel de Ville, designed by Jean Bullet. The little garden is said to be of the same date, reputedly by André Le Nôtre.

A sunken square lawn is edged with narrow beds and on either side is a raised oval bed with carpet bedding of begonias and sedums flanked by cones of clipped yew. Statues ornament the centre of the raised beds and on each side are superb bronze urns. The formal garden is edged with narrow beds behind hedges of dwarf box, where rows of standard roses are underplanted with informal summer bedding schemes. On the far side from the cathedral, beyond a screen of pleached limes, is a shady grove with a 19th-century bandstand. The garden is beautifully kept.

Open: All year, daily, 8am to sunset

Further information from:
place Parmentier, 18000 Bourges
Tel: 02 48 57 80 00

Nearby sights of interest:
Cathédrale de Saint-Etienne; the
city of Bourges.

5 *Bourges: Jardin des Prés-Fichaux*

Location: On the northern edge of the centre of the city

Even in France, with its strong 20th-century tradition of the visual arts, gardening has remained largely uninfluenced by the avant garde. The Jardin des Prés-Fichaux was laid out in the 1920s to the designs of Paul Marguerita. It is formal in design but there is much originality in the interpretation of the traditional language of symmetry. On entering the main entrance in the Carrefour de l'Odéon the first sight is of a pair of lombardy poplars which frame a view of the gardens. These are common enough trees in the open landscape but treated in such an architectural fashion in a city park they have a dramatic presence. The central axis of the garden is a huge strip of lawn flanked by roses trained on oval frames. On either side are walks between looping arcades of yew, and behind these are large beds filled with box elder (*Acer negundo* 'Variegatum') all clipped to the same height, forming an immense puffy mattress of pale foliage rising above the enclosing hedges. The gardens are finely maintained with an automatic irrigation system keeping the lawns brilliant green all year.

Arching yew hedges run along
rose beds.

Château de Brécy

Location: 24km (15 miles) NW of Caen, by the D22 and minor roads

Brécy is, to my taste, one of the most exquisite and approachable gardens in France. It has a provincial feeling and the house is a charming farmhouse that has been given the air of a château. Although the entrance forecourt is embellished with a superb arched gateway and the walls are ornamented with pilasters and urns, behind lies what must have been a farmyard. With no documentary evidence, the house has long been attributed to François Mansart. It was built in the early 17th century for Jacques le Bas, a relation of Jean de Choisy of nearby Balleroy, for whom Mansart certainly did design the château.

The garden at Brécy is Renaissance in inspiration, intimately related to the house, and harmonious in all its parts. But in some respects it differs from all known gardens of its period. It lies concealed behind the house, laid out on land that slopes upwards, giving no prospect over the rural landscape, as would have been essential in such a garden in Italy. It is disposed on five terraces starting with a pair of simple *parterres de broderie* of scrolled patterns of clipped box the width of the château. As the terraces extend up the slope they become wider. Steps lead from the parterre terrace to two further with lawns and simple topiary, followed by a pair of narrow terraces. The garden bristles with stone ornament – urns, crouching lions, garlands of flowers, and pilasters. Such a quantity of ornament could easily become excessive but here, so harmoniously related is it to the overall architectural conception that it has an air of inevitable calm.

Open: Easter to Oct, Tue, Thu and Sun, 2.30–6.30pm; other times by appointment

Further information from:
4480 Saint-Gabriel-Brécy
Tel: 02 31 80 11 48
Fax: 01 47 38 10 62

Nearby sights of interest:
Bayeux (Tapisserie de la Reine Mathilde); Caen (Abbaye aux Hommes); sites of World War II Normandy landings.

A simple parterre of scrolled box spreads out on the terrace below the walls of the château.

7 *Caen: Jardin des Plantes*

Location: In the centre of the town

Open: All year, daily, 8am to sunset

Further information from:
5 place Blot, 14000 Caen
Tel: 02 31 86 28 80

Nearby sights of interest:
Caen (Abbaye aux Hommes); Bayeux (Tapisserie de la Reine Mathilde); sites of World War II Normandy landings.

The Jardin des Plantes at Caen started in 1736 as the Institut Botanique of the university. Although it became a public garden in 1829 it has continued to have a botanical role. The old botanic garden is seen, with its neatly arranged order beds, near the entrance, but is by no means exclusively botanical: ornamental blocks of bedding plants flank a gravel path which run up to the entrance of the Institut Botanique. The order beds include a collection of species of the grass family (Gramineae), several of which, such as Italian millet (*Setaria italica*) with its striking almost black bottle-brush seedheads, make beautiful garden plants. There is also a display of the native flora of Normandy.

From the entrance to the garden the ground slopes upwards, with paths winding enticingly into woodland. Different sites provide habitats for particular groups of planting – there is a rock garden of alpine character, a stream garden and, on the shady side of a rocky outcrop, ferns, hostas, hydrangeas, rodgersias, viburnums, and other shade-loving plants. A good collection of trees include a beautiful Austrian pine (*Pinus nigra* subsp. *nigra*). Glades in the woodland are ornamented with the occasional startling modern sculpture or brilliant beds of *mosaïculture*.

The original building of the *Institut Botanique* overlooks flower-filled beds.

Château de Canon

Location: 25km (15½ miles) SE of Caen, by the N13

There is no other garden like Canon, and few that possess
such charm. It has features that come from the tradition of
French formal gardens, a dash of the English landscape garden,
and ingredients which are unique. The estate is an ancient one
but the present appearance of château and garden is largely
due to one man, Elie de Beaumont, who came into possession
of the estate in 1768. Beaumont, a cultivated barrister with a
particular interest in gardens, included among his English
friends Horace Walpole, always at the centre of fashionable
garden thought in England.

   The garden today preserves a convincing impression of
its appearance in the late 18th century. The essential layout is
formal, with a central east-west axis uniting the house and a long
rectangular pool on the garden side. This strong axis is continued
to the east with an avenue of lime trees extending beyond the
enclosure of the *cour d'honneur*. Behind the château cross axes
plunge into shady woodland which in turn is laced with winding
walks. Open lawns on both sides of the building are embellished
with white marble busts on plinths, which gaze back admiringly
towards the château.

   On the west side, a long expanse of water – a *miroir d'eau* –
reflects both house and statues, and the chief cross axis cuts
across at the point where pool and lawn meet. This broad path
runs through woodland, with an avenue of limes and fragments
of box hedging and an eye-catcher at each end. To the south is
the Temple de la Pleureuse, a little classical temple erected in
1783 in memory of Elie de Beaumont's wife.
To the north, the Chinese pavilion is an airy
open-work building of wood painted scarlet,
which overhangs a boundary stream giving
views of grazing cattle and lovely parkland
and trees. Across the woodland to one side
of this are the Chartreuses, a series of walled
gardens linked together by arched openings,
originally used for cultivating fruit. Today
they have been largely turned over to
decorative purposes, with lively planting
that reaches its peak in late summer with
crinums, goldenrod, phlox, rudbeckias, and
cosmos lining the paths. At the end, rising
from a sea of pink dahlias, is a white marble
statue of Pomona, the goddess of fruit trees.

   The garden at Canon is one of the most
memorable and attractive gardens you will
ever come across.

Open: Easter to Jun, Sat, Sun
and holidays, 2–6pm; Jul to Sep,
daily except Tue, 2–7pm. Groups
by appointment at other times
Open: As above; groups of
20 or more only

Further information from:
4270 Mézidon-Canon
Tel: 02 31 20 05 07/
02 31 28 77 04

Nearby sights of interest:
Caen (Abbaye aux Hommes);
Bayeux (Tapisserie de la Reine
Mathilde); sites of World War II
Normandy landings.

A white marble figure of Pomona
presides over the fruit garden in
the Chartreuses.

Château de Caradeuc

Location: 30km (18½ miles) NW of Rennes, by the N137, D27 and minor roads

Open: 25 Mar to 15 Sep, daily, 9am–12.30pm, 1.30pm to sunset

Further information from:
35190 Bécherel
Tel: 02 99 66 77 76

Nearby sights of interest:
Rennes (Musée des Beaux Arts).

The huntress Diana protected by hedges and shapes of clipped hornbeam.

Caradeuc is sometimes described as *le Versailles Breton*, which is deeply misleading for there is no resemblance. The château was built in 1723 by Anne-Nicolas de Caradeuc. A formal garden was laid out at the same time as the château but it was replaced in the 19th century by a *jardin à l'anglaise*. This was superseded in the late 19th century by a revivalist formal garden.

A pair of bronze lions guards the entrance drive which leads to the *cour d'honneur*. Along the drive, pyramids of yew alternate with cushions of Portugal laurel and a statue of Philemon looks up towards the château. The parterre has yew topiary, and pools with scalloped moulding, with ribbons of yellow and red bedding roses round the edges. The far side of the château is especially decorative, with ornate stone urns of fruit and a dashing double staircase leading down to the terrace which forms one of the chief axes of the garden. To the east, the terrace continues under an avenue of beech, culminating in a giant Carrara marble figure of Louis XVI. To the west, the terrace leads into an elaborate formal garden, with parallel and cross axes animated by statues and decorative buildings, some of fine quality.

Although there are exciting moments at Caradeuc, on my visits I have been gripped by melancholy. Despite the garden ornaments and distinguished architecture there is something lugubrious about the château and gardens as a whole.

Château de Chenonceau

Location: 33km (20½ miles) E of Tours, by the D140

Open: 16 Mar to 15 Sep, daily, 9am–7pm; 16 Sep to 15 Mar, daily, 9am–4.30pm
Open: As above

Further information from:
37150 Chenonceaux
Tel: 02 47 23 90 07
Fax: 02 47 23 80 88

Nearby sights of interest:
Château de Chambord; Loches (medieval town).

The château is justly famous – a stunning Renaissance building to which, in the mid-16th century, Diane de Poitiers added a brilliant flight of fancy, a wing in the form of a galleried bridge jutting across the River Cher. Her garden was also famous, and is one of the best documented of its period. A contemporary drawing by Jacques Androuet du Cerceau shows an elaborate layout on both sides of the river, with the space divided into geometric enclosures in typical Renaissance fashion.

Although the chief pleasure garden today occupies two of the sites shown in Cerceau's drawing, flanking the *cour d'honneur* and raised on ramparts above the river, the planting and layout are wholly modern in flavour. The garden to the east, *le jardin de Diane de Poitiers*, is divided by diagonal and cruciform gravel paths into eight spaces, composed of lawns decorated with patterns of santolina. Narrow beds around the edge are filled with annuals, and standard mopheaded hibiscus planted at regular intervals. They can be admired from the terraced walk that runs round the garden. The effect is cheerful, and it has the priceless advantage of having the château close at hand, an unbeatable garden ornament. To the west, *le jardin de Catherine de Médicis* is a simpler affair with a central circular pool and segments of lawn edged in narrow beds.

Cherbourg: Parc Emmanuel Liais

Location: NW of the city centre

Open: All year, daily, 8am–7.30pm (8.30am–5.30pm in winter)

Further information from:
rue Emmanuel Liais,
50100 Cherbourg
Tel: 02 33 87 88 01

Nearby sights of interest:
Sites of World War II Normandy landings.

Like many other French ports, Cherbourg was a place of entry for plants and had a thriving botanical community. Emmanuel Liais was one of those 19th-century polymaths, a scientist by training, who took an interest in all his surroundings – including plants. This little park was his garden and his house is now a natural history museum. Liais bequeathed the estate to the city and many of the plants he grew survive. The soil is acid and the microclimate benign, and there are many plants which you would not expect to see so far north. The Chilean wine palm, *Jubaea chilensis*, widely seen in specialist collections on the Côte d'Azur, flourishes here, as does the very tender Indian evergreen *Viburnum odoratissimum*. Other rarities, or excellent specimens, are to be seen in the garden, which still has something of the agreeable character of a private collection.

Bedding plants, water, and the shade of fine trees make a typical French public garden.

12 *Jardin Public de Coutances*

Location: In the centre of the town

Open: Apr to Oct, daily,
9am–8pm (from Jul to mid-Sep
illuminations and music every
evening); Nov to Mar, daily,
9am–5pm

Further information from:
2 rue Quesnel-Morinière,
50200 Coutances
Tel: 02 33 45 17 79

Nearby sights of interest:
Coutances cathedral; sites of
World War II Normandy landings.

At a quick glance, this is just another well kept public garden. But the more one looks the more there is to admire. It is laid out on a slope with underlying traces of a good formal garden. The double stairs which lead grandly down, for example, have an Italianate air, with walls of clipped hornbeam. Below, a soaring stone obelisk is aligned with a staircase. Beds of *mosaïculture* display characters from cartoons – Minnie Mouse, Asterix, Tintin's dog Snowy, and so on. But distinguished statues also embellish the scene, such as a giant figure of Amiral Tourville (1642–1701), Maréchal de France, who gazes out contentedly over shipshape bedding. Nearby is a delightful helical hornbeam mound from the top of which are fine views.

In one corner of the garden, in the shade of a big beech, is an 18th-century cider press, which has a horse-powered apple-crusher with granite channels and a giant press. It has nothing to do with gardens but is a splendid sight.

13 *Dunkerque: Jardin du Musée d'Art Contemporain*

Location: To the north of the town centre

Open: All year, daily,
10am–7pm

Further information from:
avenue des Bains,
59140 Dunkerque
Tel: 03 28 59 21 65

Powerful contemporary sculptures animate the landscape in the grounds of the Museum of Contemporary Art.

The Museum of Contemporary Art is a striking building on the beach, overlooking a lagoon. Its surroundings, which also serve as an outdoor display area, have been adventurously landscaped. Blocks of white stone are scattered on the sand and plants are naturalistically disposed. Berberis, *Elaeagnus fortunei*, gorse, lyme grass (*Leymus arenarius*), sea buckthorn, and several willows all flourish here and show the virtues of bold clumps of plants with interesting foliage. In places they fall into naturalistic groups but here and there they are placed with greater deliberation, serving to mediate between the natural landscape and the stark modern building.

The sculptures arranged outside include a flock of model sheep, a giant flying fish of coloured metal panels, and purely abstract shapes, all of which find a sympathetic context in the seaside landscape that surrounds them. The lagoon is serpentine, making a fluent contrast to the jagged edges all around. Few people would want a garden such as this behind their house but it is an admirable setting for a modern museum, and it is most attractively related to the larger landscape.

14 *Abbaye Royale de Fontevraud*

Location: 15km (9¼ miles) E of Saumur by D947

Fontevraud was founded at the end of the 11th century to house two monastic communities, one for women and one for men. The surviving abbey church was started in the early 12th century and houses the tombs of some members of the Plantagenet royal family. Several later buildings of superb quality and distinction show the subsequent wealth and power of the abbey. During the French Revolution the abbey was closed and the buildings became a prison, which they remained until after World War II when Fontevraud was converted into a regional cultural centre.

The buildings at Fontevraud form a beautiful group and appropriate gardens have been made to embellish them. The hortulus, or kitchen garden, displays pot herbs and vegetables known to have been cultivated in the Middle Ages. The beds are decoratively enclosed in low fences of intertwined osier and all the plants have informative captions about their uses. The hortulus is near the magnificent 12th-century kitchen building which gives a particularly vivid idea of the scale of the community. Below the hortulus is a garden of useful plants – those needed in brewing, wine-making and for textiles (both dyes and fibres). At a little distance is the herbularius, or physic garden, with medicinal and aromatic plants disposed in narrow box-edged beds. Excellent labels explain the plants' uses and refer to Charlemagne's Capitulary (c800), which described 72 plants to be cultivated within his empire. Throughout these gardens there is no attempt at purist period planting. Although many authentic medieval plants are grown, and clearly labelled, a great deal of modern ones are also to be seen. The setting is exquisitely beautiful and there is much to be learned, in the most beguiling way.

A comfortable hotel in the abbey precinct, the Hôtellerie du Prieuré Saint-Lazare, the former priory building, makes an admirable place to stay.

Open: Jun to third Sun in Sep, daily, 9am–7pm; end Sep to May, daily, 9.30am–12.30pm, 2–6pm (or sunset, if earlier); closes 11 Nov, 25 Dec, 1 Jan

Further information from:
49590 Fontevraud-l'Abbaye
Tel: 02 41 51 73 52
Fax: 02 41 38 15 44

Nearby sights of interest:
Chinon (château, old town); Fontevraud (exhibitions of contemporary art).

Beds of period plants spread out below the exquisite abbey buildings.

15 Kerdalo

Location: 2km (1¼ miles) E of Tréguier, off the D786

Open: Mar to Nov, the first Sat of each month, 2–6pm; and by appointment

Further information from:
22220 Trédarzec
Tel: 02 96 92 35 94

Nearby sights of interest
Cathedral and city of Tréguier.

Boldly designed formal gardens lie below the terrace of the 17th-century manor house.

It is the site, together with the skills of the garden's maker, Prince Peter Wolkonsky, that make Kerdalo so remarkable. It lies in a valley hard by the estuary of the River Jaudy, close to the jagged coast of Brittany. The climate is mild here, with a high rainfall, although the land is subject to fierce sea winds. From 1965 onwards, Prince Wolkonsky laid out his garden, taking advantage both of the granite manor house, around which he made the more formal parts of the garden, and of the stream running down the valley to one side. The soil is acid and rich in humus, allowing the cultivation of ericaceous plants which flourish on the banks of the stream. Many tender plants relish the balmy climate, creating a vivid exotic presence. Among them are the spires of *Echium pininana*, as well as the lobster-claw plant (*Clianthus puniceus*). But there is no feeling of mere botanizing plantsmanship at Kerdalo – all these plants are woven into an enchanting landscape. It is animated, too, by delightful decorative buildings. A Chinese pagoda forms an eye-catcher at the head of a slender canal flanked with rhododendrons. From the garden front of the house, a double staircase is boldly decorated with a curvaceous pediment and giant cockle shells.

Kerdalo is one of the most beautiful gardens made in France this century – the product of the vision and creativity of an artist-gardener. But there is no solemnity about it; it sparkles with a disarming cheerfulness at every turn.

16 Château de Langeais

Location: 22km (13½ miles) SW of Tours by the N152, in the centre of the town

Open: Apr to Sep, daily, 9am–6.30pm (15 Jul to Aug, daily, 9am–9pm); Oct to 2 Nov, daily, 9am–12.30pm, 2–6.30pm; 3 Nov to Mar, daily, 9am to 12 noon, 2–5pm (closes 25 Dec)
Open: As above

Further information from:
37130 Langeais
Tel: 02 47 96 72 60
Fax: 02 47 96 54 44

Nearby sights of interest:
Châteaux of the Loire.

Hard by the banks of the Loire, the castle occupies an important strategic position and has a business-like, rather than ornamental, air to it. It was first built in the 10th century but its present appearance is almost entirely 15th-century, when it was rebuilt. It has preserved its late medieval character but the garden, enclosed by the castle walls, is wholly modern, designed by Achille Duchêne between the wars. A parterre is classical in spirit but with a vague whiff of Art Deco, with low brick walls, raised square or rectangular beds, and a fountain surrounded by slate crazy paving and geometric corner-pieces of yew.

While I would not recommend a special journey to visit this garden, it has a distinctive quality and makes a welcome adjunct to the château with its magnificent collections.

17 *Parc Oriental de Maulévrier*

Location: In the centre of Maulévrier, 13km (8 miles) SE of Cholet by the D20

Open: May to Sep, Tue to Fri, 10am to 12 noon, 2–5pm and Sat, Sun and Public Holidays, 2–7pm; Oct to Apr, daily except Mon, 2–6pm (closes 24 Dec to 31 Jan)

Further information from:
chemin des Grands Ponts, 49360 Maulévrier
Tel: 02 41 55 50 14
Fax: 02 41 55 48 89

After the opening up of Japan in 1865, Europe became gripped by a passion for the Orient. The Parc Oriental at Maulévrier was laid out between 1899 and 1910 by an architect, Alexandre Marcel. It lies in a shallow wooded valley through which flows the River Moine, which Marcel dammed to form a lake. On the banks of the lake he placed snow lanterns, copies of Khmer sculptures, a facsimile of a Khmer temple from Angkor-Wat, as well as many flowering trees and Japanese maples. The banks are also strewn with mossy rocks, and a Japanese bridge, painted oxblood red, runs over to a little island.

Marcel had been to Japan where he had studied historic gardens, and some of the symbolism he brought to Maulévrier. The pagoda garden, for example, is designed as a place of repose. There are mosses, ferns and spring-flowering trees and shrubs, while water gushing over rocks makes a soothing sound. Another part of the garden is designed to encourage meditation. It is enclosed in woodland, where the rustling leaves of trees are an aid to introspection, and pines provide scent from their resin and are also a symbol of longevity.

Owned since 1983 by the town of Maulévrier, the Parc Oriental has undergone an ambitious programme of restoration. It is now very well cared for and makes a delightful place to visit.

Mossy rocks, maples, and a snow lantern render a convincing Japanese atmosphere.

Château de Miromesnil

Location: 8km (5 miles) SW of Dieppe, by the N27 and minor roads

Open: May mid-Oct, daily except Tue, 2–6pm
Open: As above

Further information from:
76550 Tourville-sur-Arques
Tel and fax: 02 35 85 02 80

Nearby sights of interest:
Coastal scenery of the
Caux region.

The 18th-century *potager* seen in spring at the start of the vegetable growing season.

Although the art of the kitchen garden is practised, as one might expect, to a high degree in France, visitors do not often have access to a proper working *potager*. The 17th-century château at Miromesnil, made of brick and stone, lies in beautiful wooded country. It was the birthplace, in 1850, of the writer Guy de Maupassant. The kitchen garden, enclosed by 17th-century brick walls at one end of the château, is divided in four parts in the traditional way. Flowery borders line one of the central paths, and contain espaliered fruit trees and jungles of delphiniums. Beds on either side are full of the well-regimented produce of the *potager*, and ornamental borders run along the encircling walls. Although decorative, the *potager* is quite unpretentious, and in late summer when it is in full productive flow, it is a mouthwatering sight.

Those visitors interested in garden history should have a good look at the landscape to the south of the château. Here, beyond a deep terrace, are signs of informal landscaping (with a magnificent cedar of Lebanon) but there are also traces of a formal avenue disappearing into the distance. Is this the remains of some 17th-century layout contemporary with the château?

19 *Mont-Saint-Michel: Jardin du Cloître*

Location: 22km (13½ miles) SW of Avranches, by the N276 and the D75

Open: May to Sep, daily, 9am–5.30pm; Oct to Mar, daily, 9.30am–4.30pm

Further information from:
Abbaye de Mont-Saint-Michel, 50116 Le Mont-Saint-Michel
Tel: 02 33 89 80 00
Fax: 02 33 70 83 08

In purely horticultural terms I would not be justified in including this little garden. However, the site is so astonishing, the garden so unexpected, and the views so exquisite, as to make it worth visiting. Besides, you will be filled with a self-righteous sense of achievement when you have made the exhausting climb to your goal. Mont-Saint-Michel is one of the busiest tourist sites in France – if you go in the middle of August, be warned. When you arrive on the island do not follow the crowds along the main street, which is lined with shops and restaurants, but take any of the alleyways leading uphill. It is a stiffer walk, but much quicker.

The cloister garden is at the highest part of the abbey. Its double row of thin granite columns and pointed limestone arches date from the 13th century. In the centre, a square pool is edged with box, and a lawn is surrounded by beds of informal planting – achilleas, artemisias, ferns, hostas, and roses. All this is modern; few of these plants were known in medieval gardens. On one side a giant view overlooks the salt marshes below – one of the loveliest sights in France.

Inauthentic but enchanting – plants glimpsed among the cloisters.

Le Bois des Moutiers

Location: 7km (4¼ miles) SW of Dieppe, by the D15

Open: 15 Mar to 15 Nov, daily, 10 to 12 noon, 2–6pm

Further information from:
76119 Varengeville-sur-Mer
Tel: 02 35 85 10 02
Fax: 02 35 85 46 98

Nearby sights of interest:
Coastal scenery of the
Caux region.

In the one estate of Le Bois des Moutiers, still owned and excellently maintained by the Mallet family, several exceptional features are to be found. At its heart is a remarkable Arts and Crafts house designed by Sir Edwin Lutyens – one of his few designs outside England. With Gertrude Jekyll, Lutyens also laid out a beautiful formal garden near the house. And, on the other side of the house, the Mallet family created a woodland garden.

Guillaume Mallet, who came from a Huguenot banking family, met Lutyens through an interest he shared in theosophy with Lutyens's wife Emily, and commissioned the house. It was built on an eminence at the head of a valley leading down to the sea – "Oh Emy," wrote Lutyens to his wife Emily, "it is so lovely here, so quiet and delicious . . . and the smells are all so good. You will come here one day." The Impressionist painter Claude Monet also loved the place, painting views of the valley with an intense patch of blue sea in the distance.

The white garden is centred on the west gable of the house.

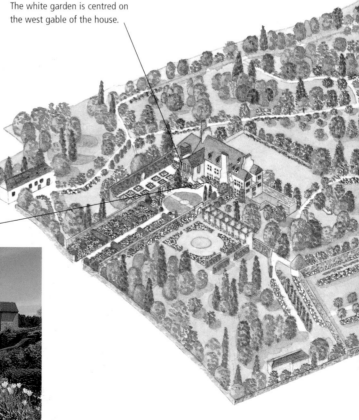

A pair of deep mixed borders form an axis linking the village street to the entrance of the house.

The woodland garden is under-planted with ferns, irises, and *Gunnera manicata*.

In late May or early June the woods are ablaze with magnificent rhododendrons.

From 1898 to 1904 Lutyens worked on the building of the house and garden layout, and Jekyll executed planting plans. Although there have been many changes to the planting, what may be seen today is an excellently preserved example of their partnership. The visitor approaches the house from the west, entering an exhilarating *enfilade* of garden rooms. The first enclosure is a paved white garden with a pattern of square box-edged beds filled with 'Iceberg' roses, 'White Triumphator' lily-flowered tulips, the white form of *Dicentra spectabilis*, and white hydrangeas. In corners at the far end from the house are two sitting areas whose design and detailing show Lutyens at his best. A low semicircular wall of horizontally laid tiles is capped with a stone moulding to form a seat. This half-encloses a circle of paving at a slightly higher level than the surrounding ground from which a semicircular stone step gives access. In the heat of the summer these cool, shady retreats provide perfect places from which to admire the surroundings. Yew hedges enclose the white garden on two sides, and one is clipped into sweeping indentations. An archway in the wall connects with the *enfilade*. This opening, a perfect Norman arch emphasized by a pattern of radiating tiles embedded in the surrounding wall, leads to the entrance courtyard on the south side of the house. Here a pair of box spheres on low box hedges stand at the head of a pair of deep borders, which lead away to the village street. A broad path

The east gable of the house – a lively and decorative design rising above simple yew hedges.

between the borders is laid in a basketweave pattern of bricks, and stucco walls backing the borders are capped with tiles. The borders are divided into compartments by buttresses of clipped yew, and the planting is dominated by white, grey, and purple. Substantial shrubs of silver *Elaeagnus commutata*, purple-leaved *Berberis thunbergii atropurpurea*, rhododendrons, and roses are underplanted with herbaceous plants – hostas, irises, Jacob's ladder, lilies, *Thalictrum aquilegiifolium*, and tulips.

From the far end of the flower borders, the house assumes its full decorative impact. It is asymmetrical and its harmony comes from the sympathetic use of materials (tiled roof, Caen stone dressings, roughcast stucco) and the repetition of some of the same materials used in the garden architecture. On the east side of the entrance courtyard, the *enfilade* continues with a path leading to a pergola of oak beams and brick columns, planted with roses, clematis, and *Vitis coignetiae*. The path continues past a garden of magnolias to another typical Lutyens building: an open round summerhouse of brick and tile, which links two paths approaching each other at an awkward angle.

On the north side of the house, where the land slopes away towards the sea, the garden has a wholly different character. The house on this side has a severer, less playful, aspect. An open expanse of grass lies before it and paths lead down on either side into dense woodland. Superb rhododendrons, many of them dating from Guillaume Mallet's plantings of almost a hundred years ago, create extraordinary ramparts of colour in the spring. Other distinguished acid-loving flowering shrubs ornament the woodland – camellias, enkianthus, eucryphias, and pieris – and many decorative trees such as *Nyssa sylvatica* and Japanese maples.

The estate organizes excellent conducted tours of house and garden for groups of visitors – the house can only be visited in this way, and the interior is vital to an appreciation of Lutyens's whole concept. The garden may be glimpsed from many of the windows, while from the immense windows of the double-height music room there are magnificent views northwards across the woodland garden to where, on a fine day, you can see the patch of intense blue sea that Monet admired so much.

One of the beautiful gateways in the west-east enfilade, with patterns of tiles in the stucco.

The Jekyllesque white garden, a flowery parterre at the west end of the house.

Open: All year, daily, 8am–8pm (closes 5.30pm in winter)

Further information from: route Saint-Joseph-de-Porterie, 44000 Nantes
Tel: 02 40 41 98 55
Fax: 02 40 41 59 51

Nearby sights of interest: Nantes (Musée des Beaux Arts, château).

21 *Nantes: Parc de la Beaujoire*

Location: On the northern edge of the city

This garden had its origins in the Floralies exhibition of 1971 and is a bold attempt to create a completely modern public park. The first part of the garden consists of a large collection of roses – 1,400 varieties – almost entirely modern cultivars. Many of the climbing varieties are supported on curious iron and wood structures like upside-down lamp standards. The majority of the roses are the repeat-flowering kind and perform throughout the summer. Impeccable lawns are watered by an automatic irrigation system, and paths are finely paved in granite.

At the far end of the rose garden, the land descends to a large rock garden which runs down to the banks of the River Erdre. Among the rocks are attractive plantings of herbaceous perennials, with some effective colour associations – orange *Helenium* 'Moerheim Beauty' with purple-leaved sage and a dusty red form of *Phygelius capensis*, for example. By the banks of the river is a striking modernist garden with blocks of different heathers – each block of a single variety – all of the same height but with subtle contrasts of flower and foliage. Eighty varieties are used, to flower at different times throughout the year. Also by the river bank is a *Collection Nationale Spécialisée* of magnolias – 200 species and cultivars – a superb sight in the spring.

Waves of bearded irises precede an explosion of roses.

Nantes: Jardin des Plantes

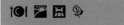

Location: In the centre of the city

Open: All year, daily, 8am to sunset (closes 9pm in summer)

Further information from:
rue Stanislas Baudry,
44000 Nantes
Tel: 02 40 41 98 55
Fax: 02 40 41 59 51

Nearby sights of interest:
Nantes (Musée des Beaux Arts, château).

The city of Nantes has an important place in the history of plant introductions in France. As early as 1726, Louis XV charged all naval captains to bring back from their voyages any plants of interest. Plants arriving at Nantes were to be gathered at the Physic Garden, grown on, and sent to the Jardin du Roi in Paris. In 1791 a new garden was founded, with an interest in ornamental plants, and this in turn became the Jardin des Plantes. Although much expanded, it still incorporates the original site, now surrounded by attractive undulating ground with groups of fine trees and a network of ornamental lakes and streams.

The great attraction of the garden today is the combination of fine landscaping and the wealth of plant interest. Several glasshouses protect collections of tender plants – two cactus houses, a palm house which accommodates substantial trees, and an orangery with citrus plants. A botanical garden displays a systematic collection of the flora of western France. The central part of the garden has many outstanding trees. In a notable collection of poplars, a *Populus deltoides* is especially beautiful. A substantial grove of planes has several magnificent old *Platanus orientalis* and *P. occidentalis*. There are fine specimens of magnolia, *Carpinus betulus* var. *pyramidalis*, and *Liriodendron tulipifera*. An exceptional range of camellias, over 1,000 varieties, makes a brilliant display early in the year.

This is not merely a plant-spotter's garden; it is also a delightful place in the middle of a big city in which to walk or sit, and enjoy an admirable and beautifully cared for landscape.

Bold splashes of summer bedding glow in the shade of trees.

 ## Orléans: Parc Floral de la Source

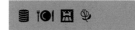

Location: 6km (3¾ miles) S of Orléans by the N20

Open: Apr to 12 Nov, daily, 9am–6pm (closes 8pm from mid-Jun to end Aug)

Further information from:
45100 Orléans
Tel: 02 38 49 30 00
Fax: 02 38 49 30 19

Nearby sights of interest:
Orléans (Musée des Beaux Arts); Château de Blois.

La Source is an old estate – the château was owned in the early 18th century by Lord Bolinbrooke, a friend of Voltaire. Its name derives from the source of the River Loiret, which springs from its well-wooded grounds. In its present form the garden was founded in 1963, although it has increased immensely in size and complexity and is now primarily a display garden – a shop window for plants and horticultural techniques. The style of planting tends towards the boldly municipal but the value of the garden lies less in aesthetics than in the range and interest of plants grown. In spring there is a fortissimo explosion of bulbs followed by a tremendous display of irises. A huge collection of chiefly modern roses starts to flower after the bedding schemes have been planted up, and continues through the summer. In autumn dahlias and chrysanthemums are a special feature. In addition to the displays of specific plants in their seasons, there is skilful grouping of trees and shrubs and well executed associations of colours.

Open: Last Sat in Apr to first Sun in Nov, Sat, Sun and Public Holidays, daily, 10am–7pm; 15 Jun to 15 Sep, daily, 10am–7pm

Further information from:
Lieu-dit Orsan, 18170 Maisonnais
Tel and Fax: 02 48 56 27 50

Nearby sights of interest:
Bourges (Cathédrale de Saint Etienne).

Simple, airy rose arbours are fashioned out of unplaned wood.

24 *Les Jardins du Prieuré Notre Dame d'Orsan*

Location: 65km (40 miles) SW of Bourges by the N144, the D940 and the D65

Interest in Medieval gardens has been growing, and there have been many attempts to recreate them. This is one of the most attractive of all recent examples. The Prieuré d'Orsan was established in the early 12th century by Robert d'Arbrissel, founder of the great abbey of Fontevraud (see p.25), although no original buildings survive here from the Middle Ages. The delightful present structure, with its elegant tower, dates from the 16th and 17th centuries.

Two architects, Sonia Lesot and Patrice Taravella, who came here in 1991, have not only restored the fine buildings but have made a garden, which is no purist recreation but a free and convincing interpretation of the Medieval spirit. Religious symbolism plays a large part in the design with, for example,

a rose garden for the Virgin Mary which does not hesitate to use modern repeat-flowering varieties. Throughout the garden, much decorative use is made of unfinished timber for fences and arbours, and wattle edging for raised beds of exactly the sort seen in Medieval miniatures. Hedges of hornbeam, beech, or hawthorn divide the spaces, and useful plants intermingle with ornamentals. Visitors are also encouraged to walk in the beautiful surrounding countryside and learn how the monastic community gathered wild plants from hedgerows and wood from the magnificent oak forests.

Although opened to the public for the first time only in 1995, the garden has already assumed an air of serene antiquity. It is a most vivid and charming evocation of the horticultural side of monastic life in the Middle Ages.

25 *Château du Pin*

Location: 25km (15½ miles) W of Angers on the N23

The château is a 12th-century fortified manor house that was rebuilt in the late Middle Ages. It is finely decorated with tall, gabled mansard windows bristling with crockets, and graceful carved stone surrounds to the ground-floor windows. The estate was bought in 1921 by Gerard Christmas Gignoux, who laid out the garden, strongly architectural in character, that visitors may see today. Its entrance lies through the house, bringing the visitor to a paved sunny terrace crowded with plants in pots – huge brugmansias, oleanders, bananas, citrus fruit with, in late summer, waves of pale blue agapanthus behind them. Steps lead down to a lower level with a lily pond and a marvellous procession of vast shapes of clipped yew which continue to the west, running parallel to the house but extending far beyond it.

The chief garden axis, however, starts with the garden door, while from the lily pond box buttresses mark the entrance to a second lily pond, surrounded by distinguished shrubs – among them *Clerodendrum trichotomum*, *Indigofera heterantha*, *Calycanthus floridus*, and *Fremontodendron californicum*. To one side, slender pools point towards a pair of Italian cypresses with beds of irises on either side. On the other, a square rose garden has a circular pool edged in lavender, beds of modern roses and an Italian cypress in each corner. Even though it is a little frayed at the edges, this garden of enclosures has great charm, and few garden visitors will fail to relish the dream-like topiary walk.

Open: Easter to Oct, Sat, Sun and Public Holidays, 2–6pm

Further information from:
49170 Champtocé-sur-Loire
Tel: 02 41 39 91 85
Fax: 02 41 39 88 41

Nearby sights of interest:
Angers (old town, château, Musée Jean Lurçat et de la Tapisserie Contemporaine).

Powerful yew topiary shapes match the liveliness of the architecture.

26 *Jardins de Plantbessin*

Location: 10km (6¼ miles) SW of Bayeux by the D73

Open: 30 May to 15 Sep, daily except Sun and Public Holidays, 2–6pm

Further information from:
14490 Castillon
Tel: 02 31 92 56 03
Fax: 02 31 22 70 09

Nearby sights of interest:
Bayeux (Tapisserie de la Reine Mathilde); sites of World War II Normandy landings.

This large and beautiful privately owned garden was created in its entirety since 1986 by its owners, Hubert and Colette Sainte-Beuve. They are also the proprietors of an excellent nursery specializing in herbaceous perennials, which is immediately next door to the garden.

Their garden is in the tradition of 20th-century gardens of compartments, in which different enclosures are given varied character by the use of fastidiously chosen plants and excellent design. A whiff of something oriental pervades one enclosure with curvaceous banks of clipped azaleas, a "poodled" cedar, swirling gravel walks, a stately *Aralia elata* 'Variegata', and a gazebo, painted oxblood red and crowned with a witch's hat roof. A herb garden, walled in yew, has raised beds, herbs planted in bold masses, and box spheres. A pergola of roses pierces a hornbeam hedge and leads to a long grassy walk, gently sloping and flanked with grandly planted borders – campanulas, dahlias, euphorbias, heleniums, lobelias, roses, and solidagos, disposed in subtle colour schemes. There are three pairs of borders, each of which is dominated by a different colour harmony – at the top they are red, yellow, and orange; in the middle, white, and cream; and at the bottom pink, purple, and red. At the back of the beds, Irish yews mark each corner – strong punctuation marks descending the slope. At the foot of the slope, an opening in a crossways yew hedge, marked by "shoulders" and clipped spheres of yew, leads down to a square garden with a lily pool edged with pots of agapanthus. At the back of it a bench is flanked by a pair of *Catalpa bignonioides*, clipped into domes. To one side a path leads to a canal, whose edges are planted with striking foliage – *Darmera peltata*, ferns, grasses, *Gunnera manicata*, hostas, and rodgersias.

Three things distinguish Plantbessin – an adventurous but unpretentious decorative sense, a very wide and well chosen range of plants, and high standards of cultivation. No gardener could fail to fall under its spell.

Foliage of striking character, often gold and variegated, fringes a slender canal.

Rennes: Parc du Thabor

Location: On the NE edge of the old city

There is plenty to admire in this particularly attractive public park. It is one of the earliest municipal parks in France, founded in 1802, and landscaped in 1865 by Denis Bühler. The entrance from the Rue Martenot is especially impressive, a monumental stone stairway leading up to a broad amphitheatre of steps with a sparkling cascade under old conifers.

The site is high and airy, with undulating land and several decorative buildings. A huge orangery looks out over formal gardens with pools and fountains, palms in *caisses de Versailles*, and exuberant bedding schemes. To one side is a large formal rose garden, mostly of modern perpetual-flowering varieties but with some old cultivars as well.

A charming aviary, shaped like a pagoda, houses in its upper part white fan-tailed pigeons, evidently relishing their superior accommodation. In the cages below exotic birds provide a brilliant display of plumage – in every way a match for the bedding schemes seen elsewhere in the garden. Many good trees ornament the garden; although none of them are great rarities, there are excellent specimens (including a marvellous old cork oak, *Quercus suber*).

Open: All year, daily, 7am to sunset (closes 9.30pm in summer)

Further information from:
place Saint-Mélaine,
35000 Rennes
Tel: 02 99 28 55 55

Nearby sights of interest:
Rennes (old town).

A swirling pattern of summer bedding *à la mosaïculture*.

 # Parc de Richelieu

Location: 19km (12 miles) E of Loudun by the D61

These ghostly remains of the one of the great gardens of France are for connoisseurs of the curious and the atmospheric. The château, the buildings that accompanied it, and the surrounding gardens are well documented. Apart from traces of the layout, and a few subsidiary buildings, nothing remains of the fabulous estate depicted in such detail in 17th-century engravings – but what does remain still has potent force. "The most handsome and magnificent château that one could ever see", as Madame de Montpensier described it, was built for Cardinal Richelieu from 1625 onwards to the designs of the architect Jacques Lemercier. He created a garden of scarcely less splendour, in the Renaissance style, with a pattern of elaborate parterres disposed about a central axis, uniting it with the château and extending far into the surrounding landscape on either side. Three radial avenues of elms converged on an immense semicircular entrance courtyard. It was the most ambitious garden that had ever been made in France and set the model for André Le Nôtre's gigantic

Open: April, 16 Sep to Oct, Sun and Public Holidays, 10am–7pm; May to 15 Sep, daily, 10am–7pm

Further information from:
place du Cardinal de Richelieu,
37120 Richelieu
Tel: 02 47 58 10 09

Nearby sights of interest:
Richelieu (old town); Azay-le-Rideau (château); Chinon (old town, château).

schemes later in the century. The estate was something of a folly, for it was far from the centres of power and Richelieu himself rarely used it.

The château was eventually demolished in 1805 and its gardens have become a public park. The approach to Richelieu from the south east by the D749 from Châtellerault, is along the route of one of the radial avenues. The semicircular courtyard is still there, its walls and pavilions intact. The garden's central axis can be viewed from the former entrance gate. The public entrance is now in the town and takes the visitor straight to what was once the *cour d'honneur* of the château, whose site is marked by a miserable rose garden with perfunctory bedding schemes. To the north, all that remains from the original garden are a pair of grotto-pavilions with long, low pedimented roofs. Another surviving building is a delightful domed pavilion, part of one of the entrance courtyards. It now houses a collection of exhibits relating to Richelieu and his estate, among them a marvellous model of the château and its garden in their heyday.

The visitor may gain a vivid impression of the scale of the enterprise by walking along the replanted avenues. It is also essential to visit the village of Richelieu which, linked axially to the garden, was also built by the Cardinal. Also designed by Lemercier, it has a grid layout of startling modernity, with its *grande rue* still lined with miniature *hôtels particuliers*.

The 17th-century entrance gate and its flanking pavilions.

Château de Sassy

Location: 11km (7 miles) S of Argentan by the N158 and minor roads

The 18th-century château occupies a splendid position on an eminence, commanding views over the rural landscape. In the 1920s Achille Duchêne was commissioned to lay out a 17th-century style parterre on the site of a kitchen garden. Here, on the far side of a moat, crossed by a bridge, is a fortissimo *parterre de broderie* with elaborate arabesques of box. Topiary and hedges of yew give structure to the whole, and the far side of the parterre is closed by a screen of pleached lime with, at its centre, an elegant little pavilion of brick and stone flanked by tall Irish yews. It is one of the prettiest of all recreations of a *jardin à la française* – all the more unexpected for its rural surroundings.

On the drive back to Saint-Christophe-le-Jajolet there is an unforgettable view of the château and garden rising among fields.

Open: Apr to Oct, daily, 3–6pm (and morning visits by appointment for groups)
Open: As above

Further information from:
61570 Saint-Christophe-le-Jajolet
Tel and Fax: 02 33 35 32 66

Nearby sights of interest:
Caen (old town, Abbaye aux Hommes).

Thury-Harcourt: Château d'Harcourt

Location: 26km (16 miles) SW of Caen by the D562

The 17th-century château was burnt down at the end of World War II and its moated remains stand at the garden entrance. You find yourself following a broad walk which runs along the edge of a field, with sycamore and beech overhanging the path and the rural landscape of Calvados to the right. Charming as it is, you begin to wonder why on earth you have come when, suddenly, the flower garden bursts into view, revealing itself spread out at the foot of a slope. It is divided into four by wide grass paths edged with narrow borders filled chiefly with annuals, forming dazzling ribbons of colour. At each corner is a big hibiscus. The garden is enclosed by a hedge of a decorative mixture of hawthorn, hornbeam, sloe, sycamore, and Japanese quince.
On the slope leading away from the garden follow a sign saying Tunnel d'Orne. The path leads to a passage of old hornbeam arched over between two fields, and after a lengthy walk there is a sight of water glinting in the distance. Here are the poplar- and willow-shrouded banks of the River Orne. At this point the path forks and either route provides a marvellous walk along the river banks, leading back to the ruins of the château. On a weekday in September Harcourt is especially beautiful. The flower garden will be at its peak and you may find yourself quite alone in this lovely place, which is unlike any other in France.

Open: Apr and Oct, Sun and Public Holidays, 2.30–6.30pm; May to Sep, daily, 2.30–6.30pm

Further information from:
14220 Thury-Harcourt
Tel: 02 31 79 65 41

Nearby sights of interest:
Caen (old town, Abbaye aux Hommes).

The flower garden with its pattern of narrow beds of brilliant colours.

Tours: Jardin Botanique

Location: SW of the town centre

Open: Nov to Feb, daily,
7.30am–5.30pm; Mar to May,
Oct, daily, 7.30am–7pm; Jun to
Sep, daily, 7.30am–8pm

Further information from:
33 boulevard Tonnelé,
37000 Tours
Tel: 02 47 21 68 18
Fax: 02 47 37 99 46

Nearby sights of interest:
Tours (Cathédrale de Saint-Gatien,
Musée des Beaux Arts); Château
d'Azay-le-Rideau; Loches (old
town, château).

The garden was founded in 1843 and has always shown a particular interest in medicinal plants. Today it combines, most attractively, the functions of a scientific institution with those of a public park of great interest to gardeners. Over 4,000 different hardy plants are grown here, among them some remarkable old specimens. A *Ginkgo biloba*, dating from 1754, has a gnarled trunk and branches erupting almost horizontally close to the base – a tree of quite extraordinary character. A *Sophora japonica* is of similar age, and there are a beautiful old specimens of *Liriodendron tulipifera*, *Magnolia acuminata*, and *Quercus macrocarpa*. A long central walk is lined with *caisses de Versailles*, planted with bougainvilleas grown as standards. On either side, borders are filled with summer bedding schemes, and a procession of *Magnolia grandiflora* provides permanent structure. A former kitchen garden has been turned over to a collection of medicinal plants.

Among several garden buildings, the most memorable is a rustic animal house inlaid with flower pots, looking like something from Grimm's fairy tales. The central area of the garden has beautifully kept lawns and open spaces allowing fine views of the magnificent trees.

The formal plantings and rich,
contrasting tones of the Jardin
Botanique, Tours.

Château d'Ussé

Location: 35km (21¾ miles) SW of Tours by D7

The pale stone château has medieval origins but was restored in the 19th century and now presents an elaborately romantic appearance with towers, steeply pitched roofs, tall chimneys and iron finials. On the route leading up to the château there is a magnificent old cedar of Lebanon and on its far side other good trees in woodland.

The chief attraction here is the delightful *jardin à la française* spread out below the terrace that lies in front of the château. An oval pool with a jet is flanked by shaped lawns, each with a round central bed; the whole surrounded by narrow box-edged beds filled with summer bedding. All along the far side of the garden are old citrus plants (some dating from the 17th century) in white *caisses de Versailles*. Beyond this dapper formality the rural countryside rolls away into the distance, with poplars along the banks of the River Indre, burgeoning fields of sunflowers, and the gently undulating wooded landscape of the Touraine.

Open: Feb to 15 Mar, daily, 10am to 12 noon, 2–5pm; 16 Mar to Easter, daily, 9am to 12 noon, 2–6pm; Easter to 13 Jul, daily, 9am to 12 noon, 2–6.45pm; 26 Sep to 11 Nov, daily, 10am to 12 noon, 2–5.30pm

Further information from:
37420 Rigny-Ussé
Tel and Fax: 02 47 95 54 05

Nearby sights of interest:
Chinon (old town, château); Richelieu (old town); Château d'Azay-le-Rideau.

The *jardin à la française* below the castle ramparts.

Open: By appointment only

Further information from:
76119 Sainte-Marguerite
Tel: 02 35 85 12 05

Nearby sights of interest:
Coastal scenery of the
Caux region.

33 *Le Vasterival*

Location: 10km (6¼ miles) W of Dieppe by the D75

Although indubitably in France, this garden could scarcely be less French. Its creator, Princess Sturdza, is a Norwegian married to a Rumanian, and the extraordinary garden she has made is close to the English tradition of woodland gardens. The site is one of the essential keys to the garden, for it is near the sea, with a benign microclimate protected by the lie of the undulating land and by dense woodland plantings. The soil is rich acid clay, made even richer by deep leaf mould.

Princess Sturdza came here in 1957 and has made a garden unlike any other. It is naturalistic in that there are no parterres, no straight lines, no topiary, and no ornaments. It is composed of a sequence of flowing shapes, lawns sweeping among groups of plants, undulating borders boldly conceived, and the natural shapes of plants powerfully used to create the architecture of the garden. An immense range of hardy plants is grown, with several thousand species and cultivars, among which are major collections: of woody plants: cherries, dogwoods, elders, rhododendrons, maples, and viburnums; and herbaceous perennials: euphorbias, ferns, hellebores, hostas, and smilacinas – which provide the underplanting that is everywhere so skilfully deployed .

For the plant-lover Le Vasterival is a special feast but, apart from its botanical interest, the garden is also a marvellous and memorable landscape. One of its most attractive qualities is the contrast between secret passages darting off into planting of jungle-like density, and long, serene vistas across open glades. There are striking associations of plants, often carried off with dashing simplicity. Waves of *Cornus canadensis*, sparkling with the violet-blue of periwinkles; a fastigiate purple beech rising beside a golden Japanese maple; an extraordinary hummock of prostrate flowering cherry with Solomon's seal growing through its sprawling branches; a pale pink double tree peony flowering behind the toffee-coloured ragged bark of *Acer griseum*. Princess Sturdza is a practical gardener of formidable knowledge and skills. One of the best things about the guided tours, which she conducts herself, is the wealth of practical gardening lore which she dispenses. As you look about in this exquisitely kept garden in which all the plants seem bursting with vigour, you cannot doubt that she knows what she is talking about.

A glade of birches sparkling with candelabra primulas.

34 *Vernon: Château de Bizy*

Location: 2km (1¼ miles) W of the town of Vernon

The intriguing gardens at the Château de Bizy are fragmentary but delightful. They were designed at the beginning of the 18th century for the Maréchal de Belleisle, probably by André Le Nôtre's nephew, Claude Desgots. The château was destroyed during the French Revolution, but many of the garden ornaments survived and a new château in handsome, neoclassical style was built in 1858 by Baron Schickler.

A dry *bassin* with splendid rusticated urns lies on the approach from the car park to the château. Behind it, among limes and horse chestnuts, is a pool with Neptune as a centrepiece. From this point a canal leads back towards the château, ending in a pair of stone dolphins. Below them is a magnificent stone screen with niches, urns, and a grotesque winged mask which gushes water.

On one side of the château is the Promenade de Vénus, a garden of quite different character. Here are the remains of shady *bosquets* of limes, and *allées* of box, enlivened with fine statues. The Venus statue acts an eye-catcher at the end of a vista that starts with a long avenue of pleached limes linking the garden with the town of Vernon lying below it.

Open: Apr to Oct, daily except Mon, 10am to 12 noon, 2–6pm

Further information from:
27200 Vernon
Tel: 02 35 51 00 82
Fax 02 32 21 66 54

Nearby sights of interest:
Valley of the Seine.

The balustraded water garden in the central *cour d'honneur*.

Château de Villandry

Location: 15km (9¼ miles) W of Tours by the D7

Open: May to Jun, daily, 9am–7.30pm; Jul to Aug, daily, 8.30am–8pm; Sep, daily, 9am–7.30pm; Oct, daily, 9am–6pm; Nov to Feb, daily, 9am–5.30pm; Mar, daily, 9am–6pm; Apr, daily, 9am–7pm

Open: mid-Feb to Mar, daily, 9.30am–5pm; Apr to Jun, daily, 9am–6pm; Jul to Aug, daily, 9am–6.30; Sep to Oct, daily, 9am–6pm; 1–11 Nov, daily, 9am–5.30pm

Further information from:
37510 Villandry
Tel: 02 47 50 02 09
Fax: 02 47 50 12 85

Nearby sights of interest:
Château d'Azay-le-Rideau; Chinon (old town and château); Tours (Musée des Beaux Arts).

Villandry is one of those gardens visited by those who have no particular horticultural interests – it has become a tourist attraction of compelling allure, with which only Versailles (see pp.80–83) and perhaps Giverny (see p.67) can compare. It is probably the most visited garden with paying admission in France. Having said that, it is something of a miracle that it has not become hopelessly Disneyfied – it retains exactly the same character that it had when I first visited it, before it had become so immensely popular. It must be said that it is inadvisable to go there in August, at the height of the holiday season. Fortunately, because it is open all the year round, it may be visited – and immensely enjoyed – on any day of the year. In deep winter it presents a charming appearance, with the austere patterns of hedges, and topiary of box and yew, marking out the design with startling clarity, unconfused by the flowers and foliage of the growing season. It is this underlying structure that gives the garden its

The *potager* spread out like patchwork quilt on the lowest terrace.

The Jardin de Musique alongside the château is full of musical imagery.

A detail of the *potager* showing its intricate pattern of beds.

The Jardin de l'Amour on the second terrace.

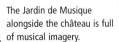

essential character and this may best be studied in the months of winter. I not only enjoy the bracing austerity of winter at Villandry, but also late spring, when there is the freshness of new foliage, or October or November when the garden is still lavishly floriferous, as well as marvellously abundant with fruit and vegetables.

Villandry occupies a fine position overlooking the River Cher, upstream from the point where it flows into the Loire. It is an ancient place – there was a great house here in the Middle Ages – but the present château was started in 1536 by Jean Le Breton, a minister at the court of François I. The garden as it is today dates from the early years of the 20th century, when the estate was bought by Dr Joachim Carvallo, who restored the château and laid out a new garden. The garden he found was a 19th-century *jardin à l'anglaise*, wildly unsuited to the character of the château, so he made a new garden honouring the spirit of the Renaissance. The garden as it exists today, with certain modifications, is exactly as Dr Carvallo left it. The ground slopes gently downwards towards the north, and has been terraced into different levels. At the lowest level is the *potager*, which consists of nine squares of identical size, each divided into an intricate, different pattern of beds edged in dwarf box. These beds are planted with two seasonal crops of vegetables, for spring and

A panorama of the gardens seen from the château terrace, with the village beyond.

summer. Although some perennials remain in place for a few years, the bulk of the vegetables are, of course, annuals, and a new plan is worked out every year. Some of the vegetables are deliberately ornamental cultivars – ruby chard, lettuces with unusually shaped or coloured leaves, parti-coloured cabbages, and so on – but much of the beauty comes from the subtle differences of leaf and colour of orderly rows of perfectly ordinary vegetables. In addition, there are two seasonal plantings of ornamental annuals or biennials, which are disposed in the narrow borders that run round each of the squares: in spring, for example, different colours of daisies (*Bellis perennis* cultivars), forget-me-nots, pansies and in summer rudbeckias, tender sages, and verbenas. At each corner of the squares graceful trelliswork arbours – *berceaux* – are festooned with roses.

The second terrace contains the formal flower gardens which flow round two sides of the *potager* at the upper level. Here the parterres are composed of patterns of box hedges, filled with annuals and punctuated with tall yew topiary shapes and leaping jets of water, which provide lively vertical notes in a chiefly horizontal plan. Some of the shapes are symbolic – in the *Jardin de l'Amour*, for example, there are shapes of horns, signifying infidelity, and fans denoting frivolous love. Such emblems were commonplace in Renaissance design. Above

In high summer brilliant bedding plants in the *potager* play their part among the beet.

this, at the third level and final level of the garden, is a complete contrast. Here a large pool is surrounded by formal lawns and smaller pools with jets of water, and edged with a walk of pleached limes. From this cool and shady vantage point, the visitor may look down on the elaborate parterres that lie spread out below.

The management and maintenance of a garden such as this is of bewildering complexity. The logistics of raising and planting the immense numbers of annual plants are awe-inspiring. The curious thing is that the place, which is flawlessly kept, has an atmosphere of marvellous serenity, with no sense of stress or strain. As for authenticity, Olivier de Serres, the 16th-century writer and gardener wrote, "It is desirable that gardens should be viewed from above, either from neighbouring buildings or from raised terraces about the parterre." The gardens at Villandry may be viewed in precisely this way and although they are far from being a purist historic reconstruction of a Renaissance layout, who can doubt that they evoke the spirit of the brilliantly patterned gardens of those times?

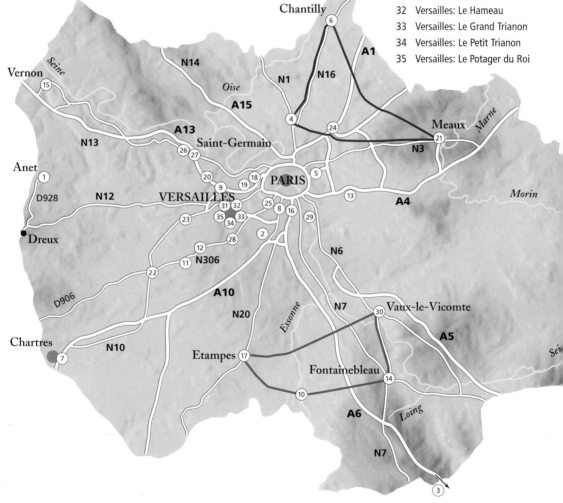

Key

═══ Motorways
─── Principal trunk highways
③ Gardens
● Major towns and cities
• Towns

Garden tours

━━ Northern tour: 6, 21, 24, 4
━━ Southern tour: 30, 14, 10, 17

Ile de France and surrounding area

Power and wealth mark the gardens of the Ile de France. The court, whether at Fontainebleau, Versailles, the Louvre, or Saint-Germain-en-Laye, was the magnet that drew the ambitious and the moneyed. The climate, a typical continental one with hot summers and harsh winters, confers no special advantage for gardeners, but the land is often well watered and fertile, as the many magnificent old woods show – Marly, Rambouillet, and many others. It is, pre-eminently, a land of great estates, and it was the homeground for André Le Nôtre. Indeed, all the major styles of French gardens, from the Renaissance to the 19th century, are represented more fully and more vividly than anywhere else in the country.

Since the 16th century, this region has reflected the most advanced taste in garden fashion in France. At Fontainebleau, François I attracted a stream of Italian artists, architects, and sculptors, from 1528 onwards, to transform the royal hunting lodge into a palace fit for a Renaissance king. At the Château d'Anet

An 18th-century pavilion overlooking the lake at the Château de Dampierre.

51

(see p.54), from 1548 onwards, Philibert de l'Orme was
the first French architect to put into practice the new
principles of Renaissance design.

The golden age of French garden design was the latter
half of the 17th century – the age of Le Nôtre. The
estates of the royal family and their courtiers have
resulted in the majority of the gardens that fascinate
visitors today. The unique complex of gardens at Versailles
are among these, but there is also Rambouillet (see
p.72), Marly (see p.71), Fontainebleau (see p.66), and
Saint-Germain-en-Laye (see p.77). The estates of the
great courtiers, such as Colbert at Sceaux (see pp.78–9)
or Fouquet at Vaux-le-Vicomte (see p.79), show the scale
of their ambitions, too. In this period every owner of a
great estate desired a great garden to match. Such estates
as Champs, Courances, Dampierre, and Saint-Cloud
vividly display the creative imagination unleashed.

The 18th-century saw the influence of the English
landscape park, although in later times many a *jardin à
l'anglaise* was restored to 17th century formality. Two
outstanding examples, however, survive to show how this
style of gardening was adapted to French taste. The Parc
Jean-Jacques Rousseau (see p.75) retains much of its Elysian
charm, and the Désert de Retz (see p.74) shows a wilder
taste for the mysterious and picturesque. These influences
continued into the following century, shaping such places
as Châteaubriand's garden in the Vallée aux Loups and
the Rothschilds' park at the Château de Ferrières.

It would be fair to say that there are no distinctively
20th-century gardens in this region. Yet the concern for
garden conservation and reconstruction of historic
layouts is a characteristic feature of the 20th century.
The Ile de France, studded with distinguished gardens,
remains one of the most attractive parts of the country.
For the garden visitor, no part of France offers such
riches in so limited an area.

Wintry weather brings out
the magic of the formal vistas
at Versailles.

Château d'Anet

Location: 20km (12½ miles) NE of Dreux by the D928, in the centre of the town

Open: Apr to Oct, daily except Tue, 2–6.30pm and Sun and Public Holidays, 10–11.30am, 2.30–6.30pm; Nov, Feb to Mar, Sat, Sun and Public Holidays, 2–5pm
Open: As above

Further information from:
28260 Anet
Tel: 02 37 41 90 07
Fax: 02 37 41 96 45

Nearby sights of interest:
Chartres (Cathédrale de Notre Dame); Versailles.

Anet is an exquisite house but its garden charms are chiefly for the historian. The house and garden were designed by Philibert de l'Orme, who built the house and garden for Diane de Poitiers, translating the latest ideas of the Italian Renaissance into a French setting. De l'Orme's design united house and garden around a single axis – a revolutionary principle in France at that time. About this axis were disposed a lavish pattern of parterres. It was almost entirely swept away after the death of Diane de Poitiers, when a grandiose Baroque scheme, either by André le Nôtre or his nephew Claude Desgot took its place. That in turn was superseded in the 19th century by English-style parkland, which may still be glimpsed to the north of the house. Of the original Renaissance scheme, there remains only de l'Orme's oval steps, leading up to a little terrace to one side of the gatehouse.

Château de Breteuil

Location: 35km (21¾ miles) SW of Paris by the A13, A12A, N10 and minor roads

Open: All year, daily, 10am to sunset; groups by appointment
Open: All year, daily, 2.30pm to sunset (opens 11am Sun)

Further information from:
Choisel, 78460 Chevreuse
Tel: 01 30 52 05 11
Fax: 01 30 52 71 10

Nearby sights of interest:
Paris; Versailles.

A stone figure finely placed between buttresses of yew.

The Château de Breteuil is in beautiful well wooded country and possesses an air of remoteness, despite being so close to Paris. The elegant brick and stone château was built early in the 17th century. An avenue leads straight towards the house and the *cour d'honneur* on the south side, where a simple garden of a pair of rectangular lawns with geometric strips of box-edged beds may be found. Behind the house, continuing the axis by the entrance avenue on the other side, is a *jardin à la française*, designed by Henri and Achille Duchêne at the turn of the century. A serene expanse of water edged with moulded stone is surrounded by strips of lawn with cushions of clipped box. To the north, the land falls away sharply – the view framed by mixed woodland pressing in on either side. Fronting the woodland are rows of yews, clipped into truncated obelisks and interspersed with statues. On the slopes below is an intricate pattern of box topiary. To one side is a memorable group of Scots pines. It is only on reaching this point that the visitor sees the ornamental axis continuing beyond the brow of the hill. The vista finally terminates in a pool and fountain, enclosed in box and hornbeam.

South east of the château is the Jardin des Princes, laid out in 1991 and named after the Princes of Wales. Beyond it the land is shaped into giant terraces. Was this the site of some great Renaissance garden contemporary with the house?

Château de Bussy-Rabutin

Location: 18km (11½ miles) SE of Montbard by the D905 and the D954

On the edge of an attractive village, the château has an especially fine position looking over rolling wooded country and scattered village houses. The moated château was built in 1649 for the Comte de Bussy-Rabutin, who was a cousin of Madame de Sévigné. It is a charmingly two-faced house: on the village side it presents a provincial façade of pale stucco flanked by sturdy pepperpot towers; the entrance side, however, is much grander, with rich Renaissance stone decoration of pilasters, pediments, and niches. To the south east of the château the garden is built on a spacious terrace, commanding views over country and village. It is arranged as a parterre, with lawns edged in narrow beds and planted with roses and peonies. A central pool is fed by a narrow rill which carries the water from a spring in a flanking wall, ornamented with a stone figure of the Water Bearer. A long gravel walk runs along the very edge of the terrace, with classical statues and a pair of elongated stone cupolas. On the other side of the château, where the land slopes upwards, are radiating avenues of limes and a dramatic stone statue of Persephone being carried off to the underworld by Pluto.

Garden visitors should on no account miss a visit to the interior of the château, which contains exquisitely painted rooms and much else of interest. This is not a garden of overwhelming excitement but it complements the château and its surrounding landscape in a harmonious and completely irresistible way.

Open: Apr to Sep, daily, visits at 10am, 11am, 2pm, 3pm, 4pm, 5pm, 6pm (closes 1 May); Oct to Mar, daily except Tue, visits at 10am, 11am, 2pm, 3pm (closes 11 Nov, 25 Dec, 1 Jan)

Further information from:
21150 Bussy-le-Grand
Tel: 03 80 96 00 03
Fax: 03 80 96 09 46

Nearby sights of interest:
City of Dijon; vineyards of the Côte d'Or.

The south façade of the château with its 17th-century pepperpot tower.

Cassan: Pavillon Chinois

Location: In the centre of the town, 36km (22¼ miles) NW of Paris by the N1

🕮 **Open:** All year, daily,
sunrise to sunset

Further information from:
rue de Beaumont,
95290 L'Isle-Adam
Tel: 01 34 69 00 52

Nearby sights of interest:
Paris.

Here is something to lift the spirit. In anonymous suburbia a glittering Chinese building rears up among trees. It is the only surviving building from a landscape park created by Pierre-Jacques Bergeret de Grancourt. He went on the Grand Tour to Italy in 1773 and came back filled with excitement for gardens that made use of water. The garden he laid out on the banks of an ornamental lake was almost entirely destroyed in World War II – except for the Chinese pavilion which has been beautifully restored. On the edge of the lake, it is raised up on a vaulted base, with the beautiful pillared undercroft visible through the stone arches. The dressed-stone quoins and fan-shaped keystones of the base of the pavilion draw their inspiration from classical architecture but the airy octagonal building above is thoroughly Chinese. The interior is exquisitely painted with *Chinoiserie* panels of birds and leafy branches in colours of faded orange and smoky blue.

The pavilion ought, of course, to be seen from the far banks of the lake, from where it would assume its full beauty. Alas, the visitor is deprived of this view, for the surroundings of the lake have been swallowed up by a maze of new houses. Even so, the pavilion is of such rare quality as to deserve a visit.

The Chinese pavilion, the central ornament of a long-lost 18th-century landscape park.

Château de Champs

Location: 20km (12½ miles) E of Paris by the A4, in the centre of the village

New towns and industrial estates, not to mention Disneyland, now dominate the Marne valley. The château and gardens at Champs are a welcome reminder of an alternative way of life. The château was built for the financier Paul Poisson in the 18th century, and the gardens were laid out in about 1710 by Claude Desgots. The Poisson family was dispossessed during the Revolution and the gardens turned over to cultivation. In 1895 they were restored by Henri Duchêne in grand Baroque style.

The entrance to the château is on the main street of the village, and although the gardens lie behind the house, the axis which links them to the château continues across the village street, piercing a semicircle of gravel edged with walks of horse chestnut, and following a lime avenue which leads to an urn. Behind the château, a terrace is ornamented with oleanders, palms and citrus fruit in *caisses de Versailles*. Steps leading down to giant box *parterres de broderie* are guarded by a pair of stone sphinxes. At the end of the parterres is a huge round pool with a centrepiece of a naked figure attacked by monsters. A cross axis has a figure at each end – Diana and Apollo – at the centre of little box-edged parterres with floriferous informal planting. Steps lead down to a broad gravel walk with palissades of horse chestnut on either side. In the far distance, at the end of an immense rectangle of lawn, is a sculpture of the Horses of Apollo.

Open: Apr to Sep, Mon to Fri, 10am to 12 noon, 1.30–5.30pm (closes 6pm Sat, Sun and Public Holidays; closes 1 May); Oct to Mar, daily, 10am to 12 noon, 1.30–4.30pm (closes 1 and 11 Nov, 25 Dec, 1 Jan)
Open: As above

Further information from:
31 rue de Paris,
77420 Champs-sur-Marne
Tel: 01 60 05 24 43
Fax: 01 64 68 26 11

Nearby sights of interest:
Paris.

In the grand manner – the central vista of the formal gardens.

 # Château de Chantilly

Location: 40km (29 miles) N of Paris by the N16, in the village of Chantilly

Chantilly is famous for its racecourse and the village is redolent of a horsy atmosphere. For lovers of gardens, André Le Nôtre's majestic formal water garden shows the essence of his genius. The Renaissance château presented no centre of gravity on which Le Nôtre could fix his design. Instead, he created a strong axis running across the entrance esplanade of the château and leading down a giant flight of steps to a terrace below. He redeployed the moats to form a rectangular pool, flanked by water parterres and crossed at its end by a vast canal for which Le Nôtre redirected the River Nonette. On the far bank of the canal, the rising ground was sculpted into a grassy amphitheatre, with "wings" of trees grouped on either side. All this survives today, serenely decorated with fine statues and urns, and looking much as Le Nôtre must have known it.

Open: Mar to Oct, daily, 10am–6pm (closes Tue, 12.45–2pm); Nov to Feb, daily, 10.30am–12.45pm, 2–5pm
Open: As above but open Tue lunchtimes

Further information from:
BP 70243, 60631 Chantilly Cédex
Tel: 03 44 62 62 62
Fax: 03 44 62 62 61

Nearby sights of interest:
Chantilly (Musée Condé, Grandes Ecuries); Beauvais (Cathédrale de Saint-Pierre); Paris (Palais de Compiègne).

On each side of the water parterres are gardens of informal character. To the east is Le Hameau, a group of half-timbered buildings erected in 1774, and thus predating the famous Hameau at Versailles. To the west, a *jardin à l'anglaise*, dating from 1820, has streams, woodland and a ruined Temple of Venus. Although both of these have their charms, it is Le Nôtre's dramatic but simple formal water garden that sticks in the mind.

Open: Apr to Oct, daily, 10am to 12 noon, 2–6pm. Open by appointment to groups at other times of the year (Tel: 02 37 36 41 39)

Further information from:
22 rue du Repos, 28000 Chartres
Tel: 02 37 34 10 78

Nearby sights of interest:
Cathédrale de Notre Dame.

 Chartres: Maison Picassiette

Location: SE of the centre of the city

In an anonymous and faintly lugubrious quarter of Chartres is one of the most extraordinary gardens in France. It is the work of Raymond Isidore (1900–64), a roadmender with a streak of pure artistic creativity. He started collecting decorative pieces of broken pottery with which he formed mosaics to decorate the walls of his little garden. The passage and outhouses leading to the garden are encrusted with vividly coloured images – birds, vases of flowers, favourite Gothic cathedrals, ships, and abstract patterns. Chairs, flower pots, and plinths fashioned of cement are also decorated with brilliant patterns. Rooms in the outhouses are similarly embellished. In the garden proper, an Eiffel Tower, with patterns of flowers, rises among petunias, and sculptures of the artist and his wife stand serenely among apple trees. There is much religious symbolism in the imagery – the Virgin Mary, a shepherd gazing towards a star, and so on. It would be wrong to dismiss all this as naïve kitsch, for there is true artistry in the inspired use of the broken fragments, which are arranged in patterns of delightful virtuosity and inventiveness. The whole effect is enchanting – like drinking half a bottle of champagne rather quickly.

Skilfully fashioned mosaics of broken china lavishly decorate the garden walls.

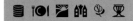

Maison de Châteaubriand

Location: 13km (8 miles) S of Paris, by the N306

In the romantically named Vallée aux Loups the romantic writer François-René de Châteaubriand came to live in 1807. Here, in *ma chère vallée*, as he called it, he cultivated his garden and planted many trees in which he took a devoted interest.

Châteaubriand's charming house and woodland garden have been finely restored, making not only a delightful place to visit but one that powerfully evokes the writer's life and character. A long wooded drive winds gently uphill from the entrance, coming soon to a turreted house which looks down a long, broad, grassy valley, densely planted with trees on either side. A path leads down one side of the valley with fine individual specimens of trees, some of which survive from Châteaubriand's time. In the woods is the Tour Velleda, a two-storey tower in which Châteaubriand had his writing room, which can be admired through the glazed door. On the way back to the house there are more outstanding trees – including some cedars of Lebanon, planted by the writer and now immense specimens. Because of financial problems, Châteaubriand was forced to sell his beloved estate in 1818 – "of all the things that fled from me, it is the only one that I regret".

Open: Apr to Sep, daily except Mon, 10am to 12 noon, 2–6pm; Oct to Dec, Feb to Mar, daily except Mon, 2–5pm
Open: As above

Further information from:
87 rue de Châteaubriand,
92290 Chatenay-Malabry
Tel: 01 47 02 58 61
Fax: 01 47 02 05 57

Nearby sights of interest:
Paris; Versailles.

Romantically placed among superb trees – a perfect writer's retreat.

Arboretum National de Chèvreloup

Location: N of the Château de Versailles, on the Saint-Germain-en-Laye road

This arboretum is an exhilarating place of unique historic interest, as well as being a fine collection of trees. It is part of the old royal estate of Versailles and was acquired by Louis XIV in 1699. In 1759 Bernard de Jussieu arranged plantings grouped according to his system of botanical classification. Trees planted by him still survive, including a beautiful *Sophora japonica*, which was raised from the first seeds sent to Europe from China in 1747. After a period of neglect from 1940 onwards, Chèvreloup became part of the Muséum National d'Histoire Naturelle. The trees are labelled, with special panels directing visitors to noteworthy specimens. Although there is no obvious attempt at landscaping, there are some finely placed groups of trees. Here visitors may learn about, and admire, some exceptional tree specimens.

Open: Apr to 15 Nov, Sat, Sun, Mon and Public Holidays, 10am–5pm. Groups by appointment at other times

Further information from:
30 route de Versailles,
78150 Rocquencourt
Tel: 01 39 55 53 80
Fax: 01 39 54 74 97

Nearby sights of interest:
Saint-Germain-en-Laye;
Versailles; Paris.

10 *Château de Courances*

Location: 61km (31 miles) S of Paris, by the A6 and the D372

Open: Apr to Oct, Sat, Sun and Public Holidays, 2–6.30pm; also open on weekdays (except Wed) to groups of not less than 20 by appointment

Open: As above

Further information from:
91490 Courances
Tel: 01 40 62 07 62
Fax: 01 47 05 04 89

Nearby sights of interest:
Forêt de Fontainebleau.

The garden at Courances is among the most attractive, and best loved, in France. Although its ingredients may be fairly easily described, it is the atmosphere of the place that constitutes its magic. This comes at least in part from the fact that it is still a privately owned estate – it has not fallen into the dead hands of a committee. It also possesses the power to exert its charms in very different circumstances. I have been there in the pouring rain, almost alone, and it was extraordinarily beautiful; on my last visit, on a Sunday on an Indian summer day in September, it was thronged with visitors clearly having a marvellous time.

The château dates from the 16th century but it was largely rebuilt in the 17th century by Claude Gallard, who also laid out the formal gardens. Contemporary engravings show how he

Two elegant pavilions guard the entrance to the château.

A box *parterre de broderie* lies below the southern façade of the château.

Water is harnessed to decorative purposes all over the gardens.

The southern façade of the château reflected in the giant canal.

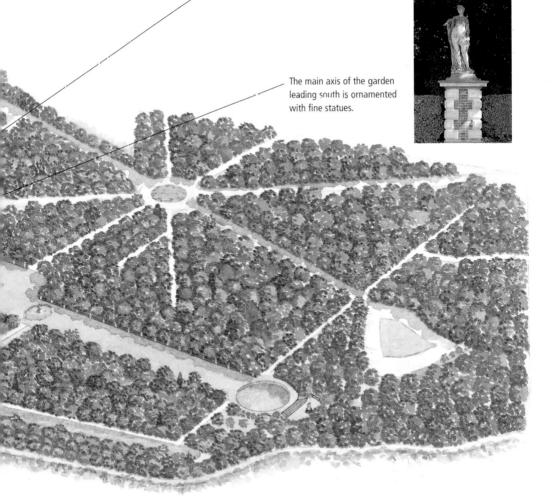

The main axis of the garden leading south is ornamented with fine statues.

61

established the unifying central axis, running north-south and aligned with the entrance drive and the centre of the château. On the south side, enclosed by the moat, is a *parterre de broderie*, and beyond it to one side, woods are laced with *allées*. All these essential features may be seen today.

The estate remained in the Gallard family until it passed by marriage to the Marquis de Nicolay who was guillotined in 1794. His widow and son stayed until 1830 and for forty years the château was empty, until it was bought by Baron de Haber, an ancestor of the present owner. A vivid glimpse of it in its period of decay is given by Jules Le Coeur, who visited it with the painters Renoir and Sisley in 1866: "such a beautiful abandoned château . . . surrounded by water and not kept up, gradually subsiding like a sugar-lump melting away in a damp corner." Haber restored the château and gardens, giving the latter the informal landscape style of the *jardin à l'anglaise*. Just before the outbreak of World War I, the Marquis de Ganay, Haber's son-in-law, commissioned Achille Duchêne to restore the garden to something resembling its 17th-century appearance. It is to him that we owe the essential layout of the garden today.

Water is the key to Courances. Not only is the land permeated by springs, but the River Ecole skirts the western boundary of the gardens and provides water for a great canal. Water, and its effects on the growth of trees, is immediately apparent at the entrance to the château. From the village street a magnificent double avenue of planes leads straight as an arrow towards the

The Japanese garden with maples and flowering shrubs reflected in a pool.

cour d'honneur of the château. These great trees, planted in 1782, are a foretaste of the multitude of splendid trees that are to be found in the garden. Between the two rows of trees are a pair of slender canals forming, with the avenue, a strong axis centred on the château that is continued on its other side.

Below the windows of the south front of the château and enclosed by the moat, lies a *parterre de broderie*, planted by Duchêne and replanted again in 1954. It was a rule of classical French garden design in the 17th century that the decorative elements should become less elaborate as they extended from the house, and this elegant but modest parterre is a perfect prelude for the simplicity of what is seen beyond. On the far side of the moat a huge rectangle of water continues the vista. At a certain point the vista narrows, creating a false perspective and making it seem even more extensive. It culminates in a figure of Hercules overlooking a circular pool. In the woods to the west of this lies the great canal, edged with broad grass walks and hedges of box. At an angle to it is a smaller stepped canal which descends in gentle falls towards the central axis. Apart from one or two ornaments, this part of the garden depends wholly on water, grass, trees, and hedges.

East of the château, on the banks of a shapely pool, a Japanese garden is laid out with crystalline water on which an island of brilliant green turf seems to float. Yews are clipped into a rounded shape and Japanese maples spread their branches across the water. A fine *Liquidambar styraciflua* gives a vertical emphasis and everywhere there is the attractive foliage of herbaceous perennials. A decorative building, a former fulling mill, makes a picturesque contribution. It has something of the air of Marie-Antoinette's Hameau at Versailles – but seen through eastern eyes.

Water gushes out of a fish's mouth, feeding a canal.

The key to the spirit of the garden – avenues of trees darkly reflected in placid water.

 ## *Domaine de Courson*

Location: 35km (21¾ miles) SW of Paris by the A10

Open: Times may vary; ring for recorded information about opening hours
Open: As above

Further information from:
Domaine de Courson
Tel: 01 64 58 90 12
Fax: 01 64 58 97 00

Nearby sights of interest
Chartres (Cathédrale de Notre Dame); Paris; Versailles.

The château at Courson was acquired by a cousin of Napoléon's, who commissioned L-M Berthault to lay out a park behind the château. In 1860 the brothers Bühler enlarged the lake and added many trees; later, between 1920 and 1950, the owner Comte Ernest de Caraman added a collection of rhododendrons. The work has continued apace, with contemporary landscape architects enriching the planting. Despite the many hands involved, the park's most striking quality is one of harmony. Around the banks of the lake, fine specimens of beech, planes, Scots pines, and swamp cypresses provide a protective canopy for the later plantings of ornamental trees and shrubs – among them maples, dogwoods, oaks, and magnolias. Although there are decorative plantings of herbaceous perennials, it is the woody plants that are the outstanding feature. Courson is also famous for the *Journées des Plantes*, in May and in October, at which nurseries and garden suppliers expose their wares and many other events of interest to gardeners take place.

Château de Dampierre

Location: 35km (21¾ miles) SW of Paris by the N118, the N306 and the D58

Open: Apr to mid-Oct, daily, 11am–6.30pm
Open: Same days as for the gardens, 2–6.30pm

Further information from:
78720 Dampierre
Tel: 01 30 52 53 64
Fax: 01 30 52 51 21

Nearby sights of interest:
Versailles; Paris.

The 17th-century château reflected in Le Nôtre's water garden.

The moated château dates from the 1680s when it was built for the Duc de Chevreuse to the designs of Jules Hardouin-Mansart. It has a fine position in the centre of the village, and the axis which unites its components runs northwards across the village high street. Here a balustraded screen with urns is centred on the entrance gates to the château, while above it a grassy slope rises between curving arms of horse chestnuts.

André Le Nôtre's majestic landscape adapted existing canals behind the château, and these flank the southern vista. The château looks out over rectilinear pools and lawns, and beyond to a balustraded pool where the land rises in a scalloped amphitheatre, with a stone figure of the Rape of the Sabine Women at its head. At the far end of a broad curved canal edged with more horse chestnuts a delightful pavilion provides an eye-catcher – rusticated stone is inlaid with tufa, and *putti* playing with lions or dolphins frolic about the parapet. To return, follow the northern side of the canal, which ends in the *cour d'honneur* where the arcaded ranges of outhouses are ornamented with carved heads of deer and horses. Le Nôtre's scheme fixes the château firmly in its stately landscape, while walks along the canals allow the visitor to relish the shifting views that present themselves.

Château de Ferrières

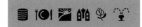

Location: 35km (21¾ miles) E of Paris, off the A4

Rothschilds in both France and England often patronized the same architects and landscape architects. Sir Joseph Paxton, who combined the two skills in a single dazzling personality, had built Mentmore in England for Baron Meyer Amschel de Rothschild between 1850 and 1855. In 1853 Baron James de Rothschild commissioned from Paxton a château and a garden at Ferrières, saying to him: "Make me a Mentmore, only grander." The house was ridiculed by contemporary French taste but later opinion has regarded it as one of Paxton's great successes.

There are formal gardens at the front of the house but the park and a lively terraced garden lie behind it. From the paved terrace running along the back of the house, a double staircase descends to a lower level. It is ornamented with yew topiary, among which are a pair of somnolent lions who scarcely glance at the park spread out before them. Paxton dammed a stream to create a vast sinuous lake, planting trees in subtle groups on the banks. There is repeat planting of many species to which he added specimens of the more distinctive 19th-century parkland trees, particularly conifers. Here are splendid examples of *Cedrus libani* subsp. *atlantica* Glauca Group, swamp cypress (*Taxodium distichum*), *Sequoiadendron giganteum*, and *Thuja plicata*.

On the way out do not miss the specimen of *Sequoiadendron giganteum*, planted by the Emperor Napoléon III in 1862. The first seeds of this great tree had only arrived nine years previously and the trees soon took Europe by storm.

Open: May to Sep, daily except Mon and Tue, 2–5pm; Nov to Apr, Sat, Sun and Wed, 2–5pm. Groups by appointment at other times

Further information from:
77164 Ferrières
Tel: 01 64 66 31 25

Nearby sights of interest:
Paris.

In front of the château a lake is subtly planted with trees.

Château de Fontainebleau

Location: 65km (40 miles) SE of Paris by the A6, in the centre of the town

Open: Spring and summer, daily, 8am–7.45pm; autumn and winter, daily, 9am–4.45pm

Open: Jun to Oct, daily except Tue, 9.30am–5pm (closes 6pm in Jul and Aug); Nov to May, daily except Tue, 9.30am–12.30pm, 2–5pm (closes 25 Dec, 1 Jan, 1 May)

Further information from:
77300 Fontainebleau
Tel: 03 60 71 50 70
Fax: 03 60 71 50 71

Nearby sights of interest:
Paris.

A pale stone 18th-century pavilion seems to float on the surface of a formal pool.

Fontainebleau is a royal palace with arguably more historic reverberations than any other in France – "la maison des siècles, la vraie demeure des rois" ("the house of centuries, truly the home of kings"), as Napoleon said. In 1528, François I commissioned the Renaissance palace that still lies at the heart of the estate. Of brick and stone, it is a beguiling mixture of fantasy and sobriety. A garden in keeping with the new château was also laid out, which was greatly extended by Catherine de'Medici, with much Italian influence, later in the 16th century. Several of its features survive to this day: the lake below the Cour de la Fontaine, the Grotte des Pins (possibly designed by Francesco Primaticcio), and the tree-lined walk leading to the Porte d'Orée.

From 1661 onwards – quite early in his career – André Le Nôtre made various designs for the garden, including a giant four-part parterre to the south east of the château, which survives today in simplified form. A square pool, with a tiered fountain, is surrounded by gravel walks and lawns with clipped cones of yew and edged in summer with bedding plants. Round the whole are stately walks shaded with pollarded limes. Le Nôtre did not find the flat site appropriate for the dramatic changes in level which he deployed so effectively at Château de Vaux-le-Vicomte (see p.79). But Napoléon loved Fontainebleau: "For me," he wrote, "my English garden is the forest of Fontainebleau." He also relished the château and the formality of the gardens, opening up the *cour d'honneur* to the west of the château which today forms the public entrance. Now, behind blue and gilt railings of Empire style, velvety lawns have cones of yew at each corner, and down the middle, leading to the famous double serpentine staircase, is a decorative parade of citrus plants in dark green *caisses de Versailles*.

Later in the 19th century, the ground to the west of the lake was landscaped in the English style, where today copies of classical statues are displayed. The horticultural charms of Fontainebleau are mostly of a historical kind but they still possess power. The gardens are open every day, free to visitors, and are much appreciated by those who live in the town, who treat them as a magnificent public amenity. This imparts an attractive air of busy-ness to the grand surroundings.

15 *Giverny: Musée Claude Monet*

Location: 4km SE of Vernon, by the D5

Open: Apr to Oct, daily except Mon, 10am–6pm
Open: As above

Further information from:
27620 Giverny
Tel: 02 32 51 28 21
Fax: 02 32 51 54 18

Nearby sights of interest:
City of Rouen; Paris; Valley of the Seine.

"I am good for nothing except painting and gardening" said the great impressionist Claude Monet. Since its restoration in the 1980s, the artist's garden at Giverny has became a major tourist attraction. Immense numbers of visitors throng to see the house and garden, both of which have much to say about the painter's life and art. Monet lived here from 1883 until his death in 1926, drawing deeply on the inspiration of his garden for his paintings, culminating in the increasingly abstract giant views of waterlilies which dominated his later years.

The garden is in two parts – the formal pattern of flower beds beneath the house, called the Clos Normand, and a water garden to which the visitor has access by passing underneath a railway line. The Clos Normand is a series of narrow parallel beds, separated by gravel paths running down from the house. This is intensely floriferous, with many annuals added to the permanent planting of herbaceous perennials, shrubs, and ornamental trees. In high summer it achieves an astonishing explosion of colour, with roses festooning archways, nasturtiums flowing over paths, foxgloves and delphiniums erupting from the beds, and sweet peas filling the air with scent. The effect is one of heady profusion rather than of the calculating harmonies of the garden designer.

The water garden, with its famous Japanese bridge draped with wisteria, has a completely different, more meditative, character. The banks of a sinuous pool are planted with azaleas, rhododendrons, and flowering cherries, and the surface of the water is splashed with waterlilies. The visitor has the feeling of having wandered into one of Monet's watery paintings. Atmosphere is all at Giverny – the garden is full of colour and alive with the material from which Monet derived his inspiration. Much is made of the authenticity of this recreation, although it must be noted that many of the plants used, especially the cultivars in the Clos Normand, were not known in Monet's time.

An explosion of roses and pelargoniums inspired the painter Monet.

Further information from:
8 rue Albert Watel,
94240 L'Haÿ-les-Roses
Tel: 01 47 40 04 04

Nearby sights of interest:
Paris.

The French art of training roses finely displayed on a trellis arbour.

Roseraie de l'Haÿ-les-Roses

Location: 8km (5 miles) S of Paris by the N7; Métro: Porte d'Italie and bus 186 (Public Holidays bus 286); RER Ligne B Bourg-la-Reine and bus 192

All gardeners should visit this marvellous rose garden. Although it contains a huge collection, it is very much a garden exhibiting that lively decorative sense which seems the essence of the French garden. Its history starts in 1892, when a retired businessman, Jules Gravereaux, bought land near the village of L'Haÿ and started to take an interest in roses, collecting them with a growing passion. He recruited the landscape architect Edouard André to lay out the first garden ever made in which roses were the only ornamental plants. By 1910, it was so famous that the village asked to change its name to L'Haÿ-les-Roses, and in 1937 the garden was bought by the local authorities.

Today it covers 1.7ha (4 acres), beautifully laid out in a pattern of beds, walks, arbours, tunnels, and ornamental trelliswork. Well over 3,000 species and cultivars are grown here, with specialist collections devoted to particular aspects of rosiculture. There are roses that were grown by the Empress Josephine at Malmaison (see p.70), wild roses, a collection showing the evolution of garden roses, and so on. To the ordinary gardener, however, the way the roses are grown, pruned and trained will be of particular interest. Many of them are beautifully arranged on trelliswork arches, in niches, or over domes, attached with slips of osier. It hardly needs saying that the essential time to visit is from early June to the middle of July – and the evening is the best time to go. The garden is now correctly known as La Roseraie du Val-de-Marne, although the old name seems to persist.

Further information from:
91150 Morigny-Champigny
Tel: 01 64 94 57 43

Nearby sights of interest:
Forêt de Fontainebleau; Versailles; Chartres (Cathédrale de Notre Dame).

Parc de Jeurre

Location: 5km (3 miles) N of Etampes, by the N20

Jeurre is an extraordinary place, whose chief claim to fame is that it gave a home to some outstanding 18th-century garden buildings. The best of these came from the nearby Château de Méréville, which was abandoned in the 19th century. Here, in the 18th century, the Marquis de Laborde had created a great landscape garden in collaboration with the artist Hubert Robert, whose marvellous paintings of the garden in its heyday give such a vivid impression of it. It was one of the wonders of its age.

After the Revolution, when the Marquis de Laborde was guillotined, the estate passed through several hands. In 1892 four of the finest buildings were bought by Henri de Saint-Léon and moved, stone by stone, to his estate at Jeurre. They may be seen today finely disposed in the park – the Rostral Column, the façade of an ornamental dairy, the Temple of Filial Piety, and a monument to Captain Cook. Saint-Léon also rescued parts of threatened great buildings and wove them into the fabric of his château. Jeurre is of real interest only to lovers of great garden buildings – and for them it is a treat.

18 *Musée Départementale Albert Kahn*

Location: Immediately W of the centre of Paris, near the Pont St-Cloud

Open: May to Sep, daily except Mon, 11am–7pm; Oct to Apr, daily except Mon, 11am–6pm

Further information from:
14 rue du Port, 92100 Boulogne
Tel: 01 46 04 52 80
Fax: 01 46 03 86 59

Nearby sights of interest:
Paris; Versailles; Saint-Germain-en-Laye.

Albert Kahn (1860–1940) was a banker burning with idealism for the brotherhood of mankind. He cultivated the friendship of like-minded contemporaries and built up an extraordinary archive of photographs. He was also mad about gardens and between 1895 and 1910 created the garden which we can see today. The entrance leads into a Japanese garden, with a stream and miniature lake whose shores are lined with beautifully laid pebbles. A bridge arches over a stream, and Japanese maples and flowering cherries are planted on the grassy terraces above the water. When the museum devoted to Kahn's work was built, some striking new features were added to the Japanese garden. Water now tumbles down a cascade from a giant cone of pebbles; a mound, with a spiral path to its centre, is covered in close-clipped azaleas. Beyond this is a formal rose garden and orchard, and a glasshouse with a magnificent interior. The remainder of the garden is informal in spirit, with paths winding among trees, a lake with rocky outcrops, a marsh garden and a woodland garden, the *forêt vosgienne*, designed to evoke memories of Kahn's native Vosges. All this forms an oasis of calm in this busy suburb of Paris.

A brilliant evocation of a Japanese garden: a scarlet bridge and scattered pebbles.

Château de Malmaison

Location: 10km (6¼ miles) W of Paris, by the the N13

Open: Apr to Sep, daily except Tue, 9.30am to 12 noon, 1.30–6pm (Sat and Sun, 10am–6.30pm); Oct to Mar, daily except Tue, 9.30am to 12 noon, 1.30–5.30pm (Sat and Sun, 10am–6pm)

Open: Apr to Sep, daily except Tue, 9.30am–12.30pm, 1.30–5.45pm (Sat and Sun, 10am–6.30pm); Oct to Mar, daily except Tue, 9.30am–12.30pm, 1.30–5.15pm (Sat and Sun, 10am–6pm)

Further information from:
avenue du Château,
92500 Rueil-Malmaison
Tel: 01 41 29 05 55
Fax: 01 41 29 05 56

Nearby sights of interest:
Paris; Versailles; Saint-Germain-en-Laye.

Topiary yew shapes echo the gables of the entrance front of the château.

"My garden is the prettiest in the world. It is more popular than my drawing-room," wrote the Empress Josephine about Malmaison. Although best known for her great rose collection, Josephine collected an immense range of plants which she exchanged with other gardens. She was also an important patron of Pierre-Joseph Redouté, who painted from plants in the Malmaison collection, producing *Les Liliacées*, held by many to be the greatest illustrated botanical book ever published.

Josephine died leaving such huge debts that the estate had to be sold. It passed from hand to hand and was sacked during the Franco-Prussian war. The château has now been restored as a museum of the First Empire, with magnificent Napoleana. However, although the garden possesses a modest collection of old roses, including a few known to Josephine, it is a pale shadow of the great garden it must have been in her day. Nonetheless, the setting and the fine château preserve some of the atmosphere of the First Empire and for plant lovers it is still holy ground – and there are additional attractions. The neighbouring Château de Bois-Préau is set in a handsome park and also houses a collection of exhibits relating to Napoléon. Another charming survival from the Empress Josephine's is next door to the Château de Malmaison at 229 bis, avenue Napoléon Bonaparte – La Petite Malmaison. It can be visited by appointment only to Count Stefan Czarnecki (tel: 01 47 49 48 15).

Domaine de Marly

Location: 16km (10 miles) W of Paris by the A13, N of Versailles

Louis XIV developed the estate of Marly as a retreat where he could relax after the rigours of court life at Versailles. He chose, in the words of Saint-Simon, "a muddy hollow, a stinking bog, avoided by the inhabitants of the neighbouring village". For his château he commissioned the architect of Versailles, Jules Hardouin-Mansart, who was also responsible for the layout of the garden. This retreat was executed on a heroic scale, costing more than any other of the king's building projects save Versailles. J B Martin's late 17th-century painting shows a great house flanked by two separate buildings of similar size. In front of them is an immense sunken pool with five pavilions on either side. Here the king entertained his intimates in the most informal style, with walks, picnics, music-making, and other distractions – invitations to such events, known as *les Marlys*, were coveted.

Marly passed into private hands during the Revolution and was pulled down. However, the giant sculpted landscape survives and it preserves an air of mysterious seclusion – a broad descending valley between high wooded hills with potent atmosphere. The essential pattern of the garden may still be seen, though it is bereft of the buildings, elaborate *bosquets*, and ornaments which would have given it intimacy. At the foot of the garden, on the main road, Louis XIV's giant *abreuvoir* (horse-trough) survives, and above it have been placed copies of the triumphant *chevaux de Marly*, a pair of spirited, leaping horses.

Open: All year, daily, sunrise to sunset

Further information from:
78160 Marly-le-Roi
Tel: 0130 61 60 00

Nearby sights of interest:
Versailles; Paris; Saint-Germain-en-Laye.

A prancing horse recalls the 17th-century glory of Marly.

Open: Summer, daily,
8am–7pm; winter, daily, 9am–5pm

Further information from:
5, place Charles de Gaulle,
77100 Meaux
Tel: 01 64 34 84 45
Fax: 01 60 23 97 52

Nearby sights of interest:
Paris.

Flowery walks and cloisters make
a perfect bishop's garden.

Meaux: Jardin Bossuet

Location: In the centre of Meaux, 54km (33½ miles) E of Paris, by the N3

Was this delightful garden designed by André Le Nôtre or was it designed by Jacques-Bénigne Bossuet, the famous 17th-century bishop of Meaux? No one knows, but it was laid out in the 17th century and still retains the essential character of that time.

The former Bishop's Palace is a jumble of buildings, built from the 15th to the 17th century. The garden is shaped like a bishop's mitre, with a cruciform pattern of paths dividing the area into four lawns, edged with narrow beds. In the middle, a pool has a vast mossy boulder and a water jet, and colourful borders line the central walk. Standard roses and cones of clipped box provide permanent planting underplanted with lavish summer bedding. Enclosing the whole area is a hornbeam hedge, between which an *allée* of pleached limes provides a secluded walk. Overlooking the garden is the bishop's writing room, where no doubt he polished the *Oraisons Funèbres*, which made him famous. Nothing could be less funereal, it must be said, than this flowery garden with its soothing, shady walks.

Open: May to Aug, daily,
6.30am–7.30pm; Sep to Oct, daily,
7am–6pm; Nov to Jan, daily,
8am–5pm; Feb to Apr, daily,
7am–6pm. (Note: Rambouillet is
an official residence of the
President of France and will be
closed when he is in residence.)
Open: Apr to Sep, daily
except Tue, 10am–11.30am,
2–5.30pm; Oct to Mar, daily
except Tue, 10am–11.30am,
2–3.30pm. The Chaumière and the
Laiterie: same as château except
close at 3.30pm in winter

Further information from:
78120 Rambouillet
Tel: 01 34 83 00 25
Fax: 01 32 83 02 49

Nearby sights of interest:
Versailles; Paris; Chartres
(Cathédrale de Notre Dame).

Château de Rambouillet

Location: 51km (31¾ miles) SW of Paris, by the A13, the A12 and the N10

Rambouillet is in the heart of hunting country. This, historically, was always the focus of the estate, which has its origins in the Middle Ages. In the early 18th century it was bought from Fleurian, Seigneur d'Armenonville, by the Comte de Toulouse, a son of Louis XIV by Madame de Montespan, and in 1783 passed to Louis XVI whose wife, Marie-Antoinette, hated it and famously remarked, "What am I supposed to do in this Gothic toad hole?" After the Revolution, Rambouillet passed into the hands of the state, where it has remained.

The gardens today present a lively mixture of styles. There are vestiges of a Baroque garden made by Fleurian d'Armenonville, traces of an informal 18th-century landscape garden and, the real goals for most garden visitors, two of the finest garden buildings in France. The Chaumière des Coquillages was built in 1778 for the Princesse de Lamballe, the young widow of the grandson of the Comte de Toulouse. It is a humble cottage, containing only two rooms, with stone walls, a steeply-pitched thatched roof, and a tall chimney. The circular entrance hall is encrusted with exquisite patterns of shells, which trace the forms of pilasters, niches, and friezes of an elaborate neoclassical interior. It was damaged during the Franco-Prussian war of 1871, but has been beautifully restored. Next door to it is the *garderobe*, a little panelled room painted with decorations of the greatest delicacy: swags, garlands, and ribbons are ornamented with birds, butterflies, flowers, and fruit. When the doors of two cupboards were opened, they revealed statues of black servants, which moved forward to proffer cosmetics to the ladies.

The second building, the *Laiterie de la Reine* (Queen's Dairy), was completed for Marie-Antoinette only months before the Revolution. Designed by the architect Jacques-Jean Thévenin, it contains two rooms – the first a domed rotunda with an inlaid marble floor and marble shelves to carry the containers for milk, cream, and cheese. Porcelain vessels were commissioned from the Sèvres factory for the dairy, among them the famous *bols seins*, supposedly modelled on the queen's breasts. The second chamber was a cooling room, with a barrel-vaulted ceiling and a grotto filling the back wall. Here a statue of Almathea sits on a rock with a goat held on a leash, drinking from the pool below.

Around about are the remnants of the early 18th-century formal gardens, with a large pool and vista extending away through the woodland. Lawns are edged with bedding schemes and gravel walks are lined with pleached limes or yews clipped into "sentry boxes". An immense building, the *bergerie*, or sheepcote, was built for Louis XVI to house a herd of Merino sheep, secretly imported from Spain. Their descendants live there to this day and the building has become the *Bergerie Nationale*, the national school of shepherds.

The Queen's Dairy, one of the most beautiful late 18th-century garden buildings.

Open: Mar to Oct; fourth Sat of the month lecture and tours at 2.30pm and 4pm. Groups by appointment at other times

Further information from:
allée Frédéric Passy,
78240 Chambourcy
Tel: 01 39 76 90 37
Fax: 01 39 76 35 39

Nearby sights of interest:
Paris; Versailles; St Germain-en-Laye.

One of several ruined buildings to be found in the *désert* or wilderness of Retz.

 # Le Désert de Retz

Location: 25km (15½ miles) W of Paris, by the A13 or the A14

One of the most mysterious, and attractive, gardens in France owes its survival to the energy of Olivier Choppin de Janvry, who first came across the Désert as an architectural student and was deeply seduced by its atmosphere. A landscape garden created in the late 18th century, it had lost all but a few of its ornamental buildings. It was threatened with inappropriate developments and Choppin de Janvry, together with Jean-Marc Heftler, was able to take it over and launch a full-scale restoration, the splendid results of which visitors may see today.

The original creator of the garden was François Nicholas Henri Racine de Monville, who made the Désert during the last years of the *Ancien Régime*, between 1774 and 1789. It gained almost immediate fame and was visited in its heyday by many distinguished garden connoisseurs. Engravings published in 1785 show an elaborate landscape studded with buildings and ornaments – among them the Ruined Column, the Temple of Pan, the Chinese House, an obelisk, and a pyramid/ice-house.

After the Revolution, Monville went to live in Paris and the estate fell into disrepair, although it remained a place of pilgrimage for many who appreciated its decaying charms, especially the Surrealists and other writers. In 1945 Cyril Connolly "fell hopelessly in love with the place" and saw "goats clattering up the beautifully undulating spiral staircase" of the Ruined Column. Today, the visitor can see a magnificently restored Column and Pyramid, a beautiful reconstructed blue and gold Tartar Tent, and work is under way on the restoration of other surviving features.

24 *Parc Jean-Jacques Rousseau*

Location: 47km (29¼ miles) NE of Paris, by the N2 and the N330

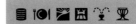

Open: Easter to Oct, Sat and Sun, 1.30–7pm; Jun to Sep, daily except Tue, 1.30–7pm. Groups in the morning by appointment

Further information from:
60440 Ermenonville
Tel: 03 44 54 01 58
Fax: 03 44 54 04 96

Nearby sights of interest:
Paris.

Many gentleman-gardeners in 18th-century France took a deep interest in the English landscape garden, which was sweeping all before it on the other side of the Channel. One of the greatest connoisseurs was the Marquis René de Girardin who created the park at Ermenonville. He inherited the estate in 1762 and proceeded to lay out a garden in the valley of the River Launette, with all manner of buildings to animate the scene. Although some of the buildings have gone and the park is disfigured by a caravan site, there are still parts where the visitor may relish exactly the feeling of Arcadian solitude which Girardin sought.

The chief surviving part of the park lies on either side of a long narrow lake, whose banks are laced with paths. On the west side it is essential to take the upper path, which leads to some of the best surviving buildings and monuments. Here, in the corner of a field, is a stone column inscribed with the words *A la Rêverie*. Further along, rising on a rocky eminence, is the Temple of Philosophy, whose columns bear the names of those philosophers admired by Girardin – Rousseau, Voltaire, Newton, and so on. The temple is deliberately left unfinished to emphasize the incompleteness of human knowledge. At the far end is one of the most famous of all 18th-century garden monuments – the tomb of Rousseau on a little island fringed with poplars. To Girardin's delight, Rousseau came to live at Ermenonville and it was here he that he died in 1778. The Ile des Peupliers and its neoclassical tombstone, inscribed with the words *Ici repose l'homme de la Nature et de la Vérité*, was designed by Hubert Robert. The banks of the lake are wooded with magnificent old beeches, limes, and planes. The monuments are rather concealed – the dolmen (a prehistoric monument of upright stones supporting a horizontal stone slab) all but hidden, the Temple of Philosophy masked by foliage, and the *Autel de la Rêverie* tucked away inconspicuously. No signs point to them, although a map is available at the entrance. Thus the visitor is encouraged to wander, explore, and make discoveries. It is especially beautiful in autumn, when a damp and misty day may encourage the melancholy introspection that 18th-century landscapers so relished.

The Temple of Philosophy on the slopes above the lake.

🌢 🍽 ✤ 🏛

🏛 **Open:** May to Aug, daily,
7am–10pm; Sep to Oct, daily,
7am–9pm; Nov to Feb, daily,
7am–8pm; Mar to Apr, daily
7am–9pm

Further information from:
92210 Saint-Cloud
Tel: 01 46 02 70 01

Nearby sights of interest:
Paris; Versailles; Saint-Germain-
en-Laye.

🍁 25 *Parc de Saint-Cloud*

Location: 9km (5½ miles) W of the centre of Paris. Métro: Pont de Sévres

Saint-Cloud has a long history of outstanding gardens. In the late 16th century Jérome de Gondi built a house with terraced gardens looking out over the Seine. In 1625 the estate was immensely expanded by Jean-François de Gondi, the first Archbishop of Paris. The garden had famous water works, almost certainly created by Thomas Francini, one of the foremost makers of ingenious garden ornaments of the day. John Evelyn visited it in 1644 and found it "rarely watered and furnished with fountains, statues and groves . . . nothing is more esteemed than the cascade falling from the great steps." In 1658 the estate was bought by Louis XIV's younger brother, Philippe de Bourbon, Duc d'Anjou, who once again embellished the gardens. It was he who commissioned a giant architectural cascade, from Antoine Le Pautre and Jules Hardouin-Mansart. It survives to this day and is one of the most extraordinary water features of any garden in France, with three gigantic ramps and bristling with sculptured ornament.

In 1665 André Le Nôtre was called in, although he was unable to impose any overall plan on an already complicated garden. He did, however, create a bold vista from the southern façade of the château, swooping down and rising again on wooded

The 17th-century cascade – the most remarkable in France.

hills – looking exactly as may be seen today. At the southern extremity of this vista is a viewing terrace, giving marvellous views of Paris. Late 17th-century engravings show a formidably complicated but enchanting layout rising in a series of terraces above the River Seine. The giant cascade forms part of a strong axis running down the hill and a pattern of parterres is linked by terraces and walks following the contours of the slopes. In the 19th century, the château retained its attractions for both emperors and kings. However, it was burnt down in 1870 and the only sign of its existence that remains is a series of cones of clipped yew marking its position. Fortunately, the garden layout triumphantly survives and retains much of the magic of its past.

26 Saint-Germain-en-Laye: Château de Saint-Germain-en-Laye

Location: 22km (13½ miles) W of Paris, by the Porte Maillot and the N186

The best approach lies to the north, where an arrow-straight avenue points directly at the château, rearing decoratively on the horizon. Saint-Germain-en-Laye was a royal palace from the early 12th century until the 17th century, when Versailles took over as the chief royal residence. After the French Revolution it became a prison, and since 1862 it has housed the Musée des Antiquités Nationales. The garden was famous in the Renaissance for grottoes with extraordinary moving figures. In one a hydraulic system caused the lady's fingers to move over the keys of an organ, producing music. Abraham Bosse's 1614 engraving shows a terraced garden descending in eight vast and intricate terraces to the Seine below. Today, only the topmost terrace survives, and this was extended by André Le Nôtre to make a great walk, 30m (98ft) wide and almost 2½km (1½ miles) long, on the escarpment overlooking the Seine. It is this that makes the most memorable feature of the garden today.

Open: All year, daily, 8am–9.30pm (closes 5pm in winter)

Further information from: place du Château, 78100 Saint-Germain-en-Laye Tel: 01 34 51 75 38

Nearby sights of interest: Versailles; Paris.

A lime walk leading off Le Nôtre's giant terrace.

27 Saint-Germain-en-Laye: Musée du Prieuré

Location: On the SW edge of the old town

I found this curious garden very attractive, although I could not defend its inclusion in this book on purely horticultural grounds. The Priory was built in the 17th century as a refuge for the poor, and in 1914 it became the home of the Symbolist painter Maurice Denis. Since 1980 it has been a museum devoted to his art and that of his circle, which included, among others, Bonnard and Vuillard. The garden preserves the character of *rus in urbe*, a private retreat from the busy-ness of the city. It descends a slope behind the house, with a herb parterre, a rose garden, and an orchard. Scattered about the garden are sculptures, some of which seem too big for their site, and thus imparting a surrealistic air. A magnificent bronze figure of a naked archer by Antoine Bourdelle, for example, dominates an enclosure at the front of the Priory.

Open: All year, daily except Mon and Tue, 10am–5.30pm (closes 6.30pm at weekends)

Further information from: 2 bis, rue Maurice Denis, 78104 Saint-Germain-en-Laye Tel: 01 39 73 77 87 Fax: 01 39 73 75 29

Nearby sights of interest: Versailles; Paris.

Open: 15 Mar to 15 Nov, Sun and Public Holidays, 2–6pm. Groups also by appointment every day except Wed

Further information from:
91940 Saint-Jean-de Beauregard
Tel: 03 60 12 00 01
Fax: 03 60 12 56 31

Nearby sights of interest:
Paris.

The quintessence of the productive *potager* in high summer.

28 *Domaine de Saint-Jean de Beauregard*

Location: 28km (17¼ miles) S of Paris, by the A10 or the N118, the D35 and minor roads

It is the 2ha (5 acre) working *potager* attached to the 17th-century château that makes Saint-Jean de Beauregard of special interest to gardeners. Enclosed in splendid 17th-century walls, it is split into four parts by two broad walks which meet at a round sunken pool at the centre. These four divisions are edged with cordons of apples or pears, while in the beds within these boundaries is a lovely profusion of fruit, vegetables, and ornamental plants.

The planting is executed with great skill and takes advantage of particular sites – for example, ferns, hellebores, hostas, and other shade-loving plants disposed in a bed running along a shady wall. As the garden comes into full productivity in the summer and autumn, there are interesting displays of the various means used for storing and preserving produce. Fresh table grapes, for example, are preserved until Christmas by the Thomery system, with the stems of individual bunches resting in glass bottles filled with the purest spring water.

Various plant festivals are held during the year. These include one devoted to herbaceous perennials in April, and one of fruit and vegetables in November.

Open: Nov to Jan, daily, 8am–5.30pm; Feb, daily, 8am–6.30pm; Mar, daily, 7am–7.30pm; Apr and Aug, daily, 7am–9.30pm; May to Jul, daily, 7am–10pm; Sep, daily, 7am–8.30pm; Oct, daily, 7am–6.30pm

Further information from:
92330 Sceaux
Tel: 01 41 61 44 85/
01 47 02 52 22
Fax: 01 46 61 21 99

Nearby sights of interest:
Paris.

29 *Parc de Sceaux*

Location: 11km S of Paris, by the N20

The estate of Sceaux was bought by Jean-Baptiste Colbert, Louis XIV's finance minister, in 1670. André Le Nôtre was called in to lay out the gardens, which were restored in the 19th century and are now a magnificent public park. Le Nôtre took advantage of the dramatic lie of the land to create one of his most memorable designs. Where the ground slopes most steeply, he made a giant cascade which tumbles down towards an octagonal pool, linked to an immense canal that runs at right angles and forms the chief axis of the composition.

Some fine garden buildings survive, in particular the Pavillon de l'Aurore, which was originally set in the kitchen garden. In this enchanting domed building Colbert used to retreat to work in the summer, and even entertained the king among the rows of fruit and vegetables. In a state of romantic decay in the

19th century, its atmosphere inspired Alain Fournier when he was writing his novel *Le Grand Meaulnes*. The beautiful Baroque Pavillon de Hanovre on the western edge of the park, facing towards the great cascade, was put here only in 1933. Designed in the late 1750s by Jean-Michel Chevotet, it was originally a wing of the Duc de Richelieu's Paris house, the Hôtel d'Antin in the Boulevard des Italiens.

The park at Sceaux is an exhilarating place in which to walk, with its vistas and surprises only gradually revealed.

30 Château de Vaux-le-Vicomte

Location: 55km (34 miles) SE of Paris, by the N6 and the N105

Vaux-le-Vicomte is the epitome of cultivated, aristocratic taste in 17th-century France. It was the creation of Nicolas Fouquet, Louis XIV's finance minister from 1653, who employed all the best artists and artisans of the day. The architect was Louis Le Vau, Charles Le Brun created the sculptures and painted the interiors, and André Le Nôtre laid out the gardens. In 1661 Fouquet entertained the king to an elaborate celebration. However, the king was shocked by the lavishness of both the château and the entertainment, and shortly afterwards Fouquet was arrested and charged with embezzlement and treason. The estate then passed from hand to hand, but in the 19th century was acquired by an industrialist, Alfred Sommier, who commissioned from Achille Duchêne a restoration of Le Nôtre's garden.

Vaux-le-Vicomte is pre-eminently a garden to walk in, for its essence lies in the subtlety of changing levels and vistas. From the steps on the garden side of the château, a dominant axis runs to the horizon, which is marked by a giant copy of the Farnese Hercules. *Parterres de broderie*, clipped yew, pools, and fountains embellish the beginning of the vista. A short distance from the château are enticing cross axes – all of which should be explored. An immense canal is discovered and on its far side the ground slopes upwards, leading to the figure of Hercules.

It is vital to visit the château as well as the garden – they were conceived at the same time and are intimately linked. From the windows of the château the garden seems to be a continuation of the exuberant decoration of the interior.

Open: Mar, daily, 11am–5pm; Apr to Oct, daily, 10am–6pm; 1–11 Nov, 11am–5pm. Note: Fountains and other ornamental water features play from Apr to Oct, on the second and last Sat of each month, 3–6pm

Open: As above

Further information from:
77950 Maincy
Tel: 01 64 14 41 90
Fax: 01 60 69 90 85

Nearby sights of interest
Paris.

The *parterres de broderie* and pyramids of clipped yew below the château walls.

Open: All year, daily, 7am to sunset

Open: 2 May to 30 Sep, daily except Mon, 9am–6.30pm; Oct to Apr, daily except Mon, 9am–5.30pm

Further information from:
78000 Versailles
Tel: 01 30 84 74 00
Fax: 01 30 84 76 48

Nearby sights of interest:
Paris; Saint-Germain-en-Laye.

31 *Versailles: Château de Versailles*

Location: 20km (12½ miles) W of Paris, by the A13

The renown of famous gardens often obscures their beauty. The first thing to say about Versailles is that it is one of the most beautiful gardens in the world, containing more distinguished works of art than any other garden and, for those who love gardens, constituting one of the greatest free treats in the world. Most visitors scarcely stray from the main thoroughfares, which means that those who are more enterprising will be rewarded with unfrequented parts of the garden, where they may be alone even at the height of the holiday season. Because it is open for so many hours every day, all through the year, it may be seen in very different circumstances of light and weather. The main axis

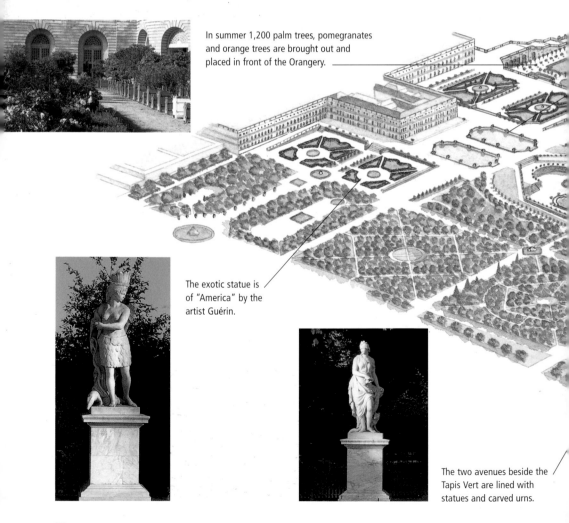

In summer 1,200 palm trees, pomegranates and orange trees are brought out and placed in front of the Orangery.

The exotic statue is of "America" by the artist Guérin.

The two avenues beside the Tapis Vert are lined with statues and carved urns.

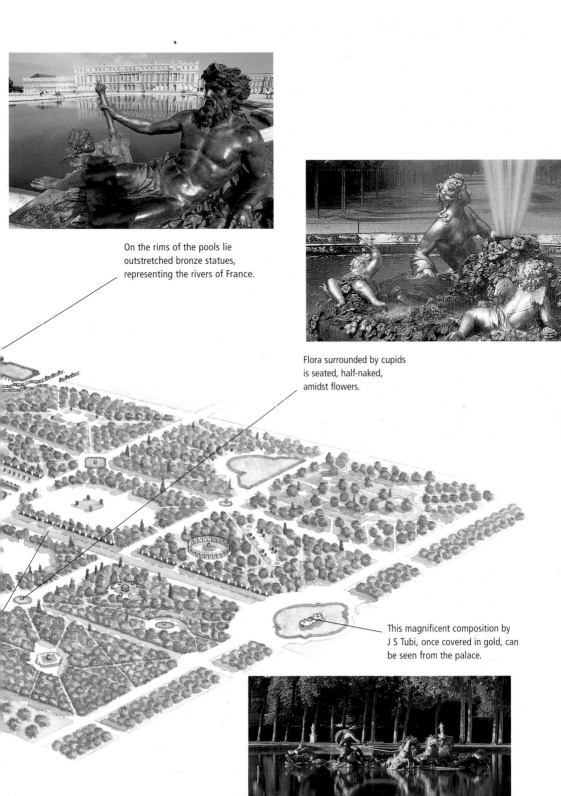

On the rims of the pools lie
outstretched bronze statues,
representing the rivers of France.

Flora surrounded by cupids
is seated, half-naked,
amidst flowers.

This magnificent composition by
J S Tubi, once covered in gold, can
be seen from the palace.

The long walk of the Allée Royale is punctuated by sculptures and vases.

The Bassin d'Apollon veiled in fountains – for lack of water the fountains rarely flow.

runs from east to west, a circumstance which must have pleased the Sun King, Louis XIV, so the rising and setting sun suffuses each end of this axis with lovely effects of light.

Versailles started as a hunting box, built by Louis XIII in 1638. A formal garden was made quite early on, with elaborate *parterres de broderie* designed by Jacques Boyceau de la Baraudière, and later in the century the house was enlarged and more land acquired. The site was scarcely propitious for garden making: Saint Simon described it as "the most sad and barren of places, with no view, no water and no woods". By the time Louis XIV transformed Versailles in the 1660s, the original garden occupied almost exactly the area of today's *petit parc*, and its westernmost boundary was marked by a *bassin* in exactly the same position as the existing Bassin d'Apollon.

The group of artists and craftsmen in charge of the new château and the garden was exactly the same as that which had made Vaux-le-Vicomte (see p.79). It was Charles Le Brun who commissioned the works of art which are still such an essential part of the gardens' beauty. He, too, worked out the iconography of the ornaments, celebrating the life of Apollo, the Sun King, with whom Louis XIV identified.

Le Nôtre designed an immense new axis running to the west, and aligned with the centre of the new château, taking advantage of the slight fall in the land to create terraces. He excavated the land to make the cruciform Grand Canal, whose east-west arm, part of the dominating vista, is no less than 1,800m (6,000ft) in length. The north-south arm, only slightly shorter, now forms a cross axis leading to the Trianon palace (see p.85). Supplying enough water for the ornamental pools and fountains at Versailles was always a problem. Attempts were made to pump it with a network of windmills from nearby springs, or to raise it from the Seine using the Machine de Marly, and there was even an attempt to reroute the River Eure by aqueducts. To this day water remains a problem, and the fountains play only on Sundays from May to October and for other special celebrations.

The *petit parc* and its surroundings were the most highly ornate part of the garden. Here was a profusion of parterres, *bosquets*, fountains, pools, and superlative urns and statues of bronze or marble. The disposition of these ingredients on either side of the central axis was not symmetrical, but the elements balance each other harmoniously. All this may be seen today, corresponding in almost every detail to late 17th-century plans of the garden, although there has, of course, been much replanting.

In 1775 and 1875 there were major replantings of the trees which
form the most important patterns of the garden. In 1990 a great
storm destroyed more than 1,300 trees. A continuous programme
of restoration is gradually returning the detail of the garden
closer to the spirit of Le Nôtre. The detail of the planting,
however, is still very often dominated by 19th-century-style
bedding schemes, even in some of the most important parterres
– such as the *parterre du midi* immediately adjacent to the
château. But in the last ten years or so this has become more
restrained than it used to be.

Le Nôtre himself was a plantsman of deep knowledge, and
rare plants in the 17th-century were coveted by all cultivated and
discerning people. In Le Nôtre's time at Versailles the parterres
sparkled with great rarities displayed like priceless jewels.
Something of this atmosphere may still be seen in the *parterre de
l'orangerie*, where a magnificent parade of tender plants in *caisses
de Versailles* are arranged every spring. They spend the winter in
Hardouin-Mansart's magnificent vaulted orangery.

All visitors to Versailles should take a walk in the town itself
and note the three streets that run up to the Place d'Armes on
the east side of the château. All three – the Avenue de Saint-
Cloud, the Avenue de Paris, and the Avenue de Sceaux – were
visible in 17th-century plans, appearing as part of the designed
approach to the château. Today they form a harmonious and
powerful link between the château and the busy life of the town.

The Bassin de Latone crowned
with Balthazar Marsy's
magnificent 1670 sculpture of
Latona and her children.

Versailles: Le Hameau

Location: On the northern edge of the gardens of Versailles

Open: All year, daily, 7am to sunset

Further information from:
78000 Versailles
Tel: 01 30 84 74 00
Fax: 01 30 84 76 48

Nearby sights of interest:
Paris; Saint-Germain-en-Laye.

Le Hameau was recently restored and has never looked more enchanting. It was built from 1783 onwards for the Queen, Marie-Antoinette, to the designs of Richard Mique. You will probably walk to Le Hameau from the Petit Trianon (see p.86), following a winding stream fringed with bulrushes and crossed by a pretty stone bridge from which you will glimpse the buildings of Le Hameau in the distance. The epitome of the picturesque, it is a rustic village grouped round a lake surrounded by woodland. A contemporary, Madame Campan, wrote: "The pleasure of wandering about all the buildings of the Hameau, of watching cows milked and of fishing in the lake enchanted the Queen."

A thatched cottage has a *potager* of tomatoes, french beans, and poppies edged in box hedges and filled with pots of scarlet pelargoniums. Other buildings are dotted along the lake's edge, most of them thatched and faced in rough stucco. In Marie-Antoinette's time the interiors were sumptuously furnished, causing visitors to gasp in amazement at the contrast with the rustic exteriors. Near the lake are some fine trees, including beautiful Scots pines, swamp cypresses by the water's edge and, overshadowing a path, a superb oriental plane. Trees, water, grass, and decorative buildings form an enchanting ensemble.

Thatched roofs and rustic woodwork at the heart of Le Hameau.

33 *Versailles: Le Grand Trianon*

Location: By car or on foot by the Grille de la Reine

Originally known as the Trianon de Porcelaine because of the glazed Delft tiles on its roof, Le Grand Trianon was built in 1671 as an elegant garden pavilion. It was replaced by the present pair of arcaded buildings, of pink and grey marble linked by a colonnade, in 1687. The gardens, originally laid out by André Le Nôtre, were modified after his death in 1700 by the architect Jules Hardouin-Mansart.

In Louis XIV's time, the garden was filled with flowers: a planting plan for one of the parterres survives, showing over 40,000 tulips, 27,000 white narcissi, and vast quantities of campanulas, pinks, valerian, violets, and other perennials. Le Nôtre wrote in 1694: "the . . . garden is filled with orange trees and flowering trees . . . flanking the parterres are arbours of pink jasmine of admirable beauty." This charming and varied mixture has been replaced by the use of bedding schemes, but the essential layout remains the same.

From the western façade of the Trianon the ground slopes down in a series of parterres marking the main axis of the garden. A secondary axis runs north and south, and, glimpsed through a gap in a lime walk at its southern end, is a view of the Grand Canal. The far end of the first axis is marked by a finely shaped pool and double cascade – trimmed in the same pink and grey marble as the house itself. The cascade is flanked by a pair of splendid winged monsters made of lead. Beyond the pool are the intensely atmospheric remains of the Trianon *bosquets* – a maze-like pattern of hedged enclosures.

The best way to enter the Grand Trianon is by the Grille de la Reine – which you may do by foot or by car. As you proceed down a broad walk, you will see fields with sheep and cattle grazing and, to the north, distinguished-looking trees – the southern edge of the Arboretum National de Chèvreloup (see p.59).

🏠 **Open:** All year, daily, 7am to sunset
🏛 **Open:** 2 May to 30 Sep, daily except Mon, 10am–6.30pm; Oct April, Tue to Fri, 10am–12.30pm, 2–5.30pm; Sat and Sun, 10am–5.30pm

Further information from:
78000 Versailles
Tel: 01 30 84 74 00
Fax: 01 30 84 76 48

Nearby sights of interest:
Paris; Saint-Germain-en-Laye.

The geometry of the French formal garden – cones of yew and patterns of box.

Versailles: Le Petit Trianon

Location: Adjacent to The Grand Trianon

Open: All year, daily, 7am to sunset

Open: 2 May to 30 Sep, daily except Mon, 10am–6.30pm; Oct to Apr, Tue to Fri, 10am–12.30pm, 2–5.30pm; Sat and Sun, 10am–5.30pm

Further information from:
78000 Versailles
Tel: 01 30 84 74 00
Fax: 01 30 84 76 48

Nearby sights of interest:
Paris; Saint-Germain-en-Laye.

The Petit Trianon, one of the most beautiful of all the buildings at Versailles, was designed by Ange-Jacques Gabriel, and the foundations were laid in 1762. There was already a garden here laid out for Gabriel's adjacent Ménagerie (long since destroyed), that had a pavilion at its heart, also designed by Gabriel – the Pavillon Français – which Louis XV and Madame de Pompadour used as a place of retreat. The *jardin à la française* surrounding the pavilion has been restored, with the original circular *bassin* at its centre, and lawns and beds with summer bedding. On either side is a lime walk with stepped hedges of hornbeam. At the centre of the pavilion is a salon with an elaborately patterned marble floor, and panelling and columns painted dove grey enriched with gilt.

Behind all this is a garden of a very different kind. Here, on ground that had been Louis XV's botanical garden, is a lake with a towering rocky grotto next to an elegant pavilion, the Belvedere. This was made between 1778 and 1779, to the designs of Richard Mique, at the request of Marie-Antoinette. The octagonal pavilion has an interior marvellously painted with panels of birds, fruit, swags of flowers, and garlands in subtle shades of grey and brown. Reflected in the placid waters of the lake, with the craggy grotto towering beside it, the pavilion makes a memorable picture of mixed elegance and wildness. A few trees survive from the botanic garden – including an extraordinary old *Sophora japonica*, with a vast trunk as gnarled as an oak.

Richard Mique's exquisite 18th-century belvedere on its island.

35 *Versailles: Le Potager du Roi*

Location: In the centre of Versailles, S of the château

Open: Apr to Nov, Wed to Sun, guided tours only at 2.30pm punctually; Jun to Sep, further guided tours on Sat and Sun, 2.30pm

Further information from:
6 rue Hardy, 78000 Versailles
Tel: 01 39 24 62 00
Fax: 01 39 24 62 01

Nearby sights of interest:
Paris; Saint-Germain-en-Laye.

Louis XIV took an intense interest in fruit and vegetables, and the former royal kitchen garden survives in a state of marvellous preservation. It was laid out from 1678 to 1683 by Jean-Baptiste de la Quintinye, who had been appointed *directeur des jardins fruitiers et potagers des maisons royales* in 1670. The garden occupies an area of 9ha (22 acres), still disposed according to its original design, with espaliered fruit trees lining the walls and paths. A huge range of vegetables and fruit is grown and sold at the market in Rungis, or to visitors to the garden. Spring for the fruit blossom, or autumn for the spectacular sight of countless different varieties of ripe fruit, are the obvious times to go. But it looks marvellous in any season. At the westernmost side, there is a view over the orderly patchwork of beds, with the château to the left and straight ahead the old houses of Versailles, with the domed cathedral rising above the rooftops.

The dome of the cathedral of St Louis rises behind the espaliered fruit trees.

Key to gardens

1	Bagatelle	9	Parc Floral de Paris
2	Parc des Buttes-Chaumont	10	Cimetière du Père Lachaise
3	Jardin Cavelier de la Salle	11	Les Serres d'Auteuil
4	Parc André Citroën	12	Les Jardins des Tuileries
5	Jardins des Halles	13	Parc de la Villette
6	Jardins des Plantes		
7	Jardins du Luxembourg		
8	Parc Monceau		

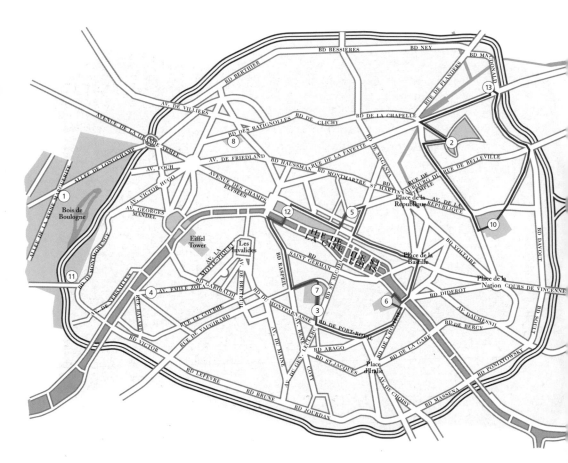

Key

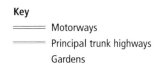

Motorways
Principal trunk highways
Gardens

Garden tours

Northern tour: 10, 2, 13
Central tour: 5, 6, 3, 7, 12

Central Paris

Paris has a wealth of public gardens, and Parisians are devoted to them. When Louis XIII founded the *Jardin Royal des Plantes Médicinales* (later to become the *Jardin des Plantes*) in 1626, he allowed the provision of a seller of lemonade for the benefit of visitors. By the second half of the 17th century, public gardens provided an essential setting for the display of *le théâtre de l'univers* – the parade of those who wished to see and be seen.

Catherine de' Medici's creation, in the 16th century, of the Tuileries gardens (see pp.100–101), immediately west of the city walls, started the westward axial march of gardens and avenues that has continued into the late 20th century. In the early 17th century, Marie de' Medici's Cours de la Reine continued the line of the Tuileries to the west, and in 1670 André Le Nôtre extended this axis with a new avenue, the Champs Elysées, which in 1724, after his death, was taken as far as the Etoile. These spectacular westward avenues were, of course, made into open countryside, and

Lively new herbaceous plantings in the Tuileries gardens.

thus linked the country with the bustling life of the city. These great public spaces still remain, as do many of the gardens attached to houses of the royal family or powerful courtiers. Henri IV's queen, Marie de' Medici, developed a new estate on the left bank of the Seine, far south of the city walls. The gardens of the Palais du Luxembourg (see p.97) today fulfill the role of a thriving public garden. In the late 18th century the Duc de Chartres made a picturesque fantasy garden at Monceau, which has become one of the city's most attractive parks, the Parc Monceau (see p.98). Bagatelle (see p.92), in the Bois de Bologne, was built in the same period, although its aura of 18th-century aristocratic elegance is now overlaid with the atmosphere of a public park of a more democratic age. From 1860 onwards Baron Haussmann transformed the appearance of the city, creating new boulevards and widening existing streets. Recognizing the need for public parks, he created the Parc des Buttes-Chaumont (see p.93), transformed the Parc Monceau, and turned over the Bois de Boulogne and the Bois de Vincennes to public use.

In the 20th century, the concern for green space in inner cities has led to the provision of yet more public parks. Under the landscape architect J C N Forestier, who was then Director General of Public Works in Paris, Bagatelle was transformed from a private estate into a public garden. Urban renewal in Paris has also allowed the creation of new public parks. A vivid example of the changing priorities is given by the history of the Citroën factory (see pp.95–5). This was opened on the Quai de Javel during World War I as an ammunition factory, and after the war became a car factory. In the 1990s, the site was ambitiously redeveloped with a lively public garden at its heart. Few cities in the world would devote precious urban space to such a public amenity.

A spectacular computer-controlled fountain at the Parc André Citroën.

🍁 *Bagatelle*

Location: On the W edge of Paris, in the Bois de Boulogne

Open: All year, daily,
8.30am–8pm (summer),
9am–5.30pm (winter)

Further information from:
route de Sèvres-à-Neuilly,
Bois de Boulogne, 75016 Paris
Tel: 01 45 01 20 50
Fax: 01 40 71 87 37

The 18th-century château
bears an inscription "Small
but appropriate".

"I walked in the park at Bagatelle, dazzled by the profusion of daisies and daffodils . . . what sorrow, I wondered, could fail to yield to the beauty of the world?" wrote Simone de Beauvoir in her memoirs. Bagatelle has enchanted many visitors and continues to do so. The miniature château was built in 1777 for the Comte d'Artois, Louis XVI's brother, to the designs of the architect François-Alexandre Belanger. The Comte d'Artois commissioned the Scottish landscape gardener Thomas Blaikie to design the park, which he did in the picturesque style, with hollows, rivers, rocky outcrops, cascades, and richly varied planting. After the French Revolution the estate was bought by Napoléon Bonaparte, but was restored to the Comte d'Artois after 1815. In 1835 it was acquired by Lord Seymour (later Marquess of Hertford), passing on his death to his illegitimate son, Sir Richard Wallace. He in turn left it to his secretary, Sir Henry Murray Scott, who sold it to the city of Paris in 1905. After 1905 the landscape architect, J C N Forestier introduced a spectacular rose garden and many beds in which flowering plants were grouped according to the colour theories of Impressionist paintings. The park you see today has been much added to since Forestier's time, although features from different periods remain, and blend harmoniously.

Traces of Blaikie's work survive in the part of the garden to the south east of the château, where formal gardens in the *cour d'honneur* and the *jardin français* exactly follow the outlines of the gardens, which were laid out when the château was built. The trees have a strongly 19th-century flavour, and fine specimens of the conifers that were so popular at that time include monkey puzzles, the rare Syrian juniper, and oriental spruce. The rose garden near the orangery, designed by Jules Gravereaux and Forestier, contains mostly modern cultivars and is beautifully maintained. Bagatelle is full of interest and deservedly popular, but it is a big garden – over 24ha (59 acres) – and even during its busiest times offers corners of delicious tranquillity.

Parc des Buttes-Chaumont

Location: On the E side of central Paris. Métro: Botzaris or Buttes-Chaumont

Open: All year, daily, 9am to sunset

Further information from:
rue Botzaris, 75019 Paris
Tel: 01 46 51 71 20

In the 1860s the hills of the Buttes-Chaumont became a public park, transformed by Baron Haussmann into an amenity for the burgeoning populace of the 19th and 20th *arrondissements*. Laid out by J-C-A Alphand and J-P Barillet-Deschamps, the park took full advantage of its dramatically hilly site. A rocky promontory rising to 50m (164ft) is crowned with a belvedere, copied from the Temple of Sibyll in Tivoli, and a giant cascade tumbles down into a lake. Paths wind about the hills and bridges of cement are given a rustic appearance, moulded to resemble the markings of bark. The slopes are clad in trees, none especially rare, although they include many excellent specimens of *Catalpa bignonioides*, several horse chestnuts, and even one or two old olive trees.

At weekends the park is agreeably full of all sorts of people enjoying themselves – excellently fulfilling the role that Haussmann intended for it.

Jardin Cavelier de la Salle

Location: Métro: Port Royal

Open: All year, daily, sunrise to sunset

Further information from:
avenue de l'Observatoire, 75006 Paris

This long and narrow garden is, in effect, a southern extension of the central vista of the Palais du Luxembourg. But it is a quite separate garden, built on land confiscated from the Carthusian monks after the Revolution. It celebrates a remarkable man, René-Robert Cavelier de la Salle, a 17th-century fur trader and explorer, who was the first man from the Old World to journey along the whole length of the Mississippi river. In April 1682, when he arrived at the Gulf of Mexico, he claimed the whole of the Mississippi valley on behalf of his king, Louis XIV, and gave it his name, Louisiana.

The little known 19th-century public garden that commemorates de la Salle is one of the finest of its period in Paris. Slender lawns run its whole length, flanked by walks of horse chestnuts. Dramatic statues, interspersed with marble columns crowned with bronze urns, run down the centre of the lawns. The walks beneath the trees are embellished on either side – and in winter illuminated – by beautiful bronze lamps mounted on handsome stone plinths. At the southern extremity of the garden, by the Place E Denis, a dazzling

The "Four Corners of the Earth" fountain by J B Carpeaux.

fountain, Les Quatre Parties du Monde, has fine sculptures by J B Carpeaux. A group of nude figures hold the universe aloft, with prancing horses and frolicking dolphins at their feet. From the surrounding pool, encircling bronze turtles spout vigorous jets of water at the figures above. Looking north from the pool is a view of the grand vista which terminates in the Palais du Luxembourg. Throughout the garden all the decorative details show craftsmanship of lovely quality – note, for example, the finely moulded surround to the pool. It is the details of this kind that add essentially to the character of the place. This is the quintessential Parisian public park.

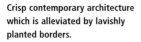

 Open: All year, daily, all the time

Further information from:
rue Leblanc, 750015 Paris

Crisp contemporary architecture which is alleviated by lavishly planted borders.

4 *Parc André Citroën*

Location: On the SW edge of the centre of Paris. Métro: Javel

This magnificent park is a rarity – a completely new piece of landscaping, covering an area of 13ha (32 acres), at the heart of an immense urban regeneration project. In 1777, on part of a former royal estate, the Comte d'Artois established here one of the earliest factories in France. During World War I, the Citroën ammunition factory opened here, turning to the manufacture of cars after the war.

Now a complex of flats, offices, shops, and other buildings has shot up, with a new park at its heart. The architect in charge was Patrick Berger, in association with the landscape architect Gilles Clément. A vast lawn edged with canals provides a restful central space, with occasional groups of trees animating the scene. On the north side are ramparts of hornbeam, interrupted at intervals by water chutes resembling the *chadars* of Mughal gardens. A paved walk runs along behind the hedges with, on its far side, a series of enclosed gardens. These gardens vary in character – some are deeply sunken so that they may be admired from above and most are planted according to a single colour scheme. The silver garden, for example, has rows of weeping silver pears (*Pyrus salicifolia* 'Pendula') on either side of a narrow wooden deck. In the centre is a gravel garden, with tufts of fescue, artemisia, thistles, and mulleins. At the far east end of the central lawn, a gently rising paved terrace has an extraordinary fountain: a geometric series of vertical water jets erupt in graceful patterns, programmed by a computer to form endless permutations of rising and falling water. On either side of it are giant glasshouses – one an exhibition space, the other housing subtropical plants. On the terrace in front are rows of crape myrtles (*Lagerstroemia indica*) in *caisses de Versailles*, and to one side is a formal grove of 5m-high (16ft) *Magnolia grandiflora* clipped into columns. When I was there, early one autumn morning, the park gradually stirred into life: people walked their dogs, a man sat down on a bench to read his paper and the park assumed its daily life – as though it had been there for a hundred years.

Jardins des Halles

Location: Métro: Halles

Open: All the time

Further information from:
rue Berger, 75001 Paris

The destruction of the great iron and glass market halls, and the building of Renzo Piano and Richard Rogers' Centre Pompidou, changed this old quarter of Paris from a commercial centre of pungent character to a tourist zone. This was the area of Paris described so powerfully by Emile Zola in his book *Le Ventre de Paris* – today it has a certain international anonymity. After twenty years, however, the public gardens that formed part of the new development have fared well, creating all sorts of leafy enclosures, flowery shrubberies, and tree-lined walks. These make a fine foil for the sharp edges and outlandish shapes of the new architecture of the Centre Pompidou and the Forum des Halles. Vine-clad iron trelliswork, hedges of yew and elaeagnus, and groves of limes, enclose occasional patches of lawn, creating the sort of nooks and crannies that the public seem to enjoy.

20th-century municipal planting on the grand scale.

6 *Jardins des Plantes*

Location: SE of the centre of Paris. Métro: Gare d'Austerlitz or Jussieu

Open: All year, daily, sunrise to sunset (8pm in summer). Glasshouses open daily except Tue, 3–5pm

Further information from:
57 rue Cuvier, 75005 Paris
Tel: 01 40 79 30 00
Fax: 01 40 79 34 84

Founded by Louis XIII in 1626 as the *Jardin Royal des Plantes Médicinales*, this was not only a place for botanical research, but also the first public garden in Paris. John Evelyn visited it quite early in its life in 1643 and found it "richly stor'd with exotic plants". From its earliest days it was a centre of botanical research, and this it remains. In the 18th century, the natural historian George-Louis Leclerc de Buffon became director of the gardens, and in 1724 the young Bernard de Jussieu brought a seedling cedar of Lebanon from the Holy Land, reputedly in his hat for lack of a pot. The tree flourished in the Jardin des Plantes and became an object of pilgrimage for Parisians. In the late 18th century, the Muséum d'Histoire Naturelle established itself here and gave a further impetus to the research which flourishes today. Jean Lamarck, whose pioneering evolutionist ideas predated those of Charles Darwin, became director of the gardens in 1774.

Today, the Jardin des Plantes combines the roles of a popular public park and a botanical research institution. It displays an immense range of plants, both hardy and tender, and many of these plants are used in the bedding displays in the *jardin à la française*, which faces the main entrance from the Place Valhubert.

On either side of a broad walk, with double avenues of pleached planes flanking it, beds are filled with summer bedding plants: 150 cultivars of dahlias, over 100 cannas and immense numbers of annuals. To the north of this, the order beds of the Ecole Botanique contain over 3,000 species of hardy plants, grouped in families (open on weekdays 8–11am, 1.30–5pm; closed Saturdays, Sundays and Public Holidays). Under glass there are several collections of plants, including 1,700 species of orchid, with over 15,000 different plants in all – one of the largest collections of tender plants in Europe.

The garden also provides a variety of entertainments of a non-horticultural kind, such as a menagerie, and many of those who frequent it regard the garden simply as an agreeable place to sit on a bench. Thus it continues the dual role as a place of recreation and of academic research that Louis XIII intended for it in the early 17th century.

Roses and dahlias underplanted with summer bedding.

Jardins du Luxembourg

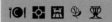

Location: Métro: Luxembourg

Open: All year, daily, 7am to one hour before sunset (opens 8am in winter)

Further information from: boulevard St Michel, 75006 Paris Tel: 01 42 34 20 00

"The appearance of the *allées* of the Luxembourg makes my heart leap", wrote Alfred de Musset, "how many times . . . have I not lain down in the shade, all filled with poetry." The Luxembourg gardens may be the place for poetic solitude but they also provide a marvellous setting for celebrations. The artist Watteau came here in the 18th century to admire the Rubens paintings in the palace and the trees in the garden, and was inspired to paint his lovely *Fêtes Galantes*.

The history of the gardens starts with Marie de'Medici who, in 1600, became the second wife of Henri IV. Twelve years later, wanting to recreate something of the ambience of her childhood home, the Pitti Palace in Florence, she commissioned a palace and garden from the architect Salomon de Brosse. The Palais du Luxembourg remained a royal palace until the French Revolution, when it became a prison, and in 1801 Napoléon Bonaparte began to use it for the Senate, which has continued using it to this day.

In the 19th century the gardens were redesigned and became a public park. Today, although the overriding atmosphere is one of 19th-century exuberance, they still bear traces of earlier times. The 17th-century grotto, designed by Alexandre Francini, still survives, although much altered and moved to a different place. The dominating southern axis and the sunken garden in front of the palace correspond to the garden's 17th-century layout. Lively summer bedding schemes, statues and urns of high quality, and shady walks of horse chestnuts and limes embellish the gardens at every turn. There is also a remarkable collection of plants. Enormous *caisses de Versailles* house many tender varieties – among them over 40 different cultivars of oleander and many varieties of citrus plants, pomegranates, and palms. An excellent collection of orchids is kept under glass, including over 400 different species and cultivars of lady's slippers (*Paphiopedilum*). Fine individual specimens of trees include some that go back to the replanting of the gardens in the early 19th century.

Today the gardens are immensely popular. One of their most attractive qualities is that they still preserve the lightheartedly festive air that so enchanted Watteau, and which he caught so vividly in his paintings.

Ebullient planting in front of the façade of the Palais du Luxembourg.

Parc Monceau

Location: NW of the city centre. Métro: Monceau

Open: All year, daily, 9am to sunset

Further information from: boulevard de Courcelles, 75008 Paris

"We strolled there until night fell, nightingales were singing in great number and a breeze blowing on beds of roses brought to us their scent and freshness", wrote the traveller John Carr in 1802. Although Parc Monceau is now a much used public park, it still preserves something of the romantic aura that charmed Carr. It was created in the 1770s for the Duc de Chartres by Louis Carrogis, known as Carmontelle, as a picturesque landscaped park filled with ornaments and decorative buildings. The landscaper Thomas Blaikie later reworked the layout just before the Revolution, after which it passed through various hands. In the 1860s, at the instigation of Georges Haussmann, it became a public park.

The gently undulating site preserves features from different periods. The colonnade came from the Valois tomb in the church of Saint Denis in Paris. A splendid Egyptian pyramid was part of Carmontelle's scheme, as were the several pieces of broken columns and fragments of masonry that lie romantically half submerged in grass. Various monuments have a distinctive 19th-century flavour, among them a fine statue of Chopin. Although the site is not large, the winding walks among groves of trees and shifting vistas across lawns, give the impression of something much larger. The entrance from the Boulevard de Courcelles has superb gilt and black railings and iron gates enriched with lovely scroll-work. Beside them, the exquisite domed and pillared lodge, designed by the neoclassical architect Claude Nicholas Ledoux, and a survivor from the Duc de Chartre's original park, finds a more mundane 20th-century use as a public lavatory.

18th-century arcadia in the centre of Paris.

Parc Floral de Paris

Location: On the E edge of Paris. Métro: Château de Vincennes

The former royal estate of Vincennes has become fragmented, and the medieval château is now detached from the Bois de Vincennes which, with an area of almost 1,000ha (2,471 acres), is still the largest public park in Paris.

The Parc Floral de Paris, on the other side of the road from the château, emerged from the Floralies exhibition held here in 1966, and now covers an area of over 30ha (74 acres). It is a display garden with large collections of particular groups of plants woven into the ornamental scheme, among them camellias, fuchsias, and peonies. There are also various thematic collections: of Mediterranean plants, and of medicinal, aromatic and culinary plants. A modern style of planting in brilliant drifts of colours is complemented by the bold use of contemporary sculpture and other garden ornaments. For those who want merely to study the plants, a weekday is best, but it is at weekends, when the park is thronged with crowds, that it assumes its most cheerful character.

Open: 31 Mar to 29 Sep, daily, 9.30am–8pm; 30 Sep to 27 Oct, daily, 9.30am–7pm; 28 Oct to 1 Mar, daily, 9.30am–5.30pm

Further information from: route des Pyramides, esplanade du Château de Vincennes, 75012 Paris
Tel: 01 43 43 92 95
Fax: 01 43 65 46 42

 # *Cimetière du Père Lachaise*

Location: E of the centre of Paris. Métro: Philippe Auguste

The former Cimetière de l'Est was founded in 1804 on land which had previously belonged to the Jesuits. Laid out by the architect Brongniart, it was planned as a completely new style of cemetery, handsomely landscaped and taking full advantage of the sloping land where the Jesuits had once had their orchards. It quickly became the most fashionable cemetery in France and today is a place of pilgrimage for visitors seeking to pay their respects to the more, or less, distinguished dead – who range from Marcel Proust to Jim Morrison.

However, this great necropolis also has a powerful character as a landscape. A vertiginous *allée* of cypresses forms a strong axis from the entrance and paths sweep off between the tombstones, which range widely in architectural styles. An outrageous sphinx with pouting lips – carved by Sir Jacob Epstein – is Oscar Wilde's memorial. Antoine-Augustin Parmentier, who promoted the fame of the potato, is commemorated by a distinguished neoclassical stone of white marble, with a frieze of potato plants. Marcel Proust is interred beneath a sleek and impassive table of black marble. A romantic weeping willow shades Chopin's tomb. All these press together on the steep hill, with many trees and the odd bright splash of colour from flowering plants.

Open: Mar to Nov, daily, 7.30am–6pm; Dec to Feb, daily, 8am–5.30pm (opens at 8.30am at weekends and Public Holidays)

Further information from: boulevard de Ménilmontant, 75020 Paris
Tel: 01 43 70 70 33

Trees and the occasional splash of colour among the tombs.

11

Les Serres d'Auteuil

Location: SW of the city centre, near the Porte d'Auteuil. Métro: Porte d'Auteuil

Open: All year, daily,
10am–7pm (closes 5pm in winter)

Further information from:
avenue de la Porte d'Auteuil,
75016 Paris
Tel: 01 46 51 71 20

Formerly part of a botanic garden founded by Louis XV, in 1898 this garden became the *fleuriste municipale* supplying thousands of tender bedding plants for the public gardens of Paris. A magnificent domed glasshouse, dating from that time, houses an impressive collection of tender plants. The lawns in front of it are superbly kept and edged in narrow borders with informal bedding schemes. This is all attractive but the real excitement comes from the outstanding trees. A rare *Ailanthus giraldii*, with intricately cut leaves, now 30m (98ft) high, spreads its branches like graceful feathers. A huge old *Sophora japonica* 'Variegata' has formed a billowing crown, its elegant foliage a ghostly silver in appearance. A magnificent specimen of *Platycarya strobilacea*, very rarely seen in gardens, was planted in 1907 and is now 20m (66ft) high. An immense and beautiful Chinese wingnut (*Pterocarya stenoptera*) is among the tallest in Europe.

In the neighbouring *jardin des poètes*, snippets of poetry inscribed on plaques relate to plants and gardens. Guillaume Apollinaire sighed in 1912, "I cannot leave you without regret, distant Auteuil, charming district of my great sadness." Today the charms of the Serres d'Auteuil are so great that they almost render inaudible the roar of the adjacent Boulevard Périphérique.

A superb *belle époque* conservatory and magnificent trees.

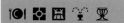

Les Jardins des Tuileries

Location: In the centre of Paris. Métro: Louvre; Palais Royal; Concorde

Open: All year, daily, sunrise to 8pm (or sunset, if earlier)

Further information from:
rue de Rivoli, 75001 Paris
Tel: 01 42 60 27 67

When the first garden was made at the Tuileries in the 16th century, this was a rural site just west of the city walls. In 1564, Catherine de' Medici, widow of Henri II, commissioned a palace from Philibert de l'Orme. Elaborate gardens were laid out and one of the gardeners who tended them was a Pierre Le Nôtre, almost certainly the grandfather of André Le Nôtre. Almost one hundred years later, André Le Nôtre was to establish for the Tuileries a layout whose essential character is visible to this day.

Napoléon Bonaparte adopted the Tuileries palace as one of his residences, and it continued as a royal palace until it was destroyed during the Franco-Prussian war. Later in the 19th century, the gardens became very popular and were embellished with sculptures by Maillol and Rodin, and with ornaments from the former royal gardens at Marly. During the 1990s, the gardens have assumed a new lease of life. Three designers – Louis Benech, Pascal Cribier, and Jacques Wirtz – have revised both the design and the planting. Benech and Cribier have laid down lawns and created borders, edging the spaces which were occupied by elaborate parterres. Wirtz has designed a garden for the Cour du Carrousel, with corridors of yew and enclosed squares of pleached limes. Stone paths set in gravel radiate from the Arc du Carrousel, continuing in the form of rounded hedges of yew in a sunken garden. The gardens remain part of the axis which Le Nôtre established over 300 years ago, but this vista now has a beginning and an end which Le Nôtre could scarcely have envisaged: to the east, I M Pei's glass pyramid forming the entrance to the Louvre, and, on the western horizon, the gigantic Arche de la Défense.

Parc de la Villette

Location: NE of the city centre. Métro: Porte de Pantin

Open: All the time

Further information from:
avenue Jean-Jaurès, 75019 Paris
Tel: 01 42 40 27 28

The site of the former cattle market, the Marché aux Bestiaux, has been transformed into an entirely new, multi-purpose public space. It is partly a cultural centre, with an emphasis on music, partly a science museum and partly a public park, designed by Bernard Tschumi.

An immense open space, surfaced in cobbles and granite paving stones, has a grand tiered pool and a fountain with pairs of lions spouting water. Behind it, the impeccably restored Grande Halle, made of iron and glass, houses all sorts of cultural activities and a restaurant. To

Brilliant colours, reflective glass and a scattering of trees.

one side are grassy spaces – much used for playing football – and a long avenue of plane trees, while startling scarlet buildings, like giant modern sculptures, ornament the perimeter. Nearby, a striking new building, the Cité de la Musique, includes a museum of music and auditoria.

By the Canal de l'Ourcq a series of gardens present different themes: a bamboo garden, a lively water garden, and a trellis garden with sculptures by Jean-Max Albert. To the north of the park, an astonishing gleaming sphere, La Géode, houses a cinema. Beyond it lies a remarkable museum of science and technology. Compared with other public spaces in Paris, the Parc de la Villette lacks the nooks and crannies which many people find congenial. Nonetheless, it has an undeniable buzz of activity which is certainly invigorating.

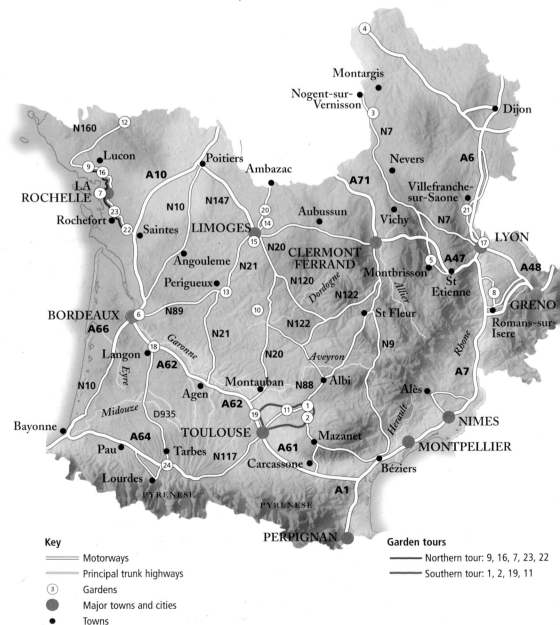

Key

═══ Motorways

─── Principal trunk highways

③ Gardens

⬤ Major towns and cities

● Towns

Garden tours

── Northern tour: 9, 16, 7, 23, 22

── Southern tour: 1, 2, 19, 11

Central & south-western France

The immense area covered in this section is one of the most attractive and varied of the whole of France. With some of the world's finest vineyards, a wide range of regional cooking, and magnificent countryside, it attracts huge numbers of visitors. The area is dominated by the Massif Central at its heart and great rivers on either side – the Garonne to the west and the Rhône to the east.

Good gardens are always historically associated with wealth. You do not find public gardens of the quality of the Jardin des Plantes in Bordeaux in poor communities. The wealth of Bordeaux comes from its position as a major port and centre of the wine trade. Private wealth, too, lies behind some of the most interesting gardens. The Haviland family, for example, owners of one of the finest porcelain factories of Limoges, created the château and park of Mont-Méry (see p.120).

The Atlantic coast south of the Loire is one of the sunniest

Charming kitsch in the Jardin Dumaine at Luçon.

parts of France. In a garden such as the Parc Floral de le Court d'Aron (see p.111), not far from the coast north of La Rochelle, many subtropical plants flourish. The vineyards of the Bordelais benefit from the benign coastal climate and long hours of sunshine. Wine growing has provided the wealth that has allowed the building of many fine houses, of which the Château de Malle (see p.119), with its delightful garden, is an outstanding example. The relatively low rainfall on the coast does not, however, make a good climate for deciduous woodland. Further inland, towards the Massif Central, the rainfall is much higher and the climate cooler. Here there are many excellent collections of trees of which the Arboretum des Barres (see p.108) is outstanding. The Parc de Mont-Méry, just one hundred years old, is full of magnificent trees, showing vividly how quickly they can grow in these conditions. Further north east, is one of the great oak forests of France, the Tronçais – which provides the timber for barrels for some of the finest vineyards.

To the south, estates and gardens show an almost Mediterranean character. The Parc Foucaud (see p.113) has a 17th-century house, with a double flight of stairs and arcaded loggia which have a distinctly Italianate quality. Around the River Rhône the Italian connection is even more pronounced. The 16th-century Château de Bastie d'Urfé (see p.108) must be among the first buildings outside Italy to be influenced by the Renaissance.

There are no formal gardens in this area on anything like the scale of the landscapes of the Ile de France. Nonetheless, the spirit of formality is to be found. The Château de Merville (see p.119), near Toulouse, has a rare garden of formal groves and *allées* dating from the early 18th century. The garden at the Manoir d'Eyrignac (see p.112) is a beautifully manicured 20th-century evocation of the ideas of 17th-century gardening.

A stately urn ornaments the Herbarium in the Jardin Public at Bordeaux.

Albi: Palais de la Berbie

Location: In the centre of the city, immediately N of the cathedral

Open: Apr to Sep, daily, 9am to 12 noon, 2–6pm; Oct to Mar, daily except Tue, 10am to 12 noon, 2–5pm

Further information from:
BP 100, 81003 Albi Cédex
Tel: 05 63 49 48 70
Fax: 05 63 49 48 88

Nearby sights of interest:
Albi (Musée Toulouse Lautrec, Cathédrale de Sainte-Cécile).

The Palais is an imposing fortified archbishop's palace, built in the 13th century, of the beautiful pink-brown brick that is such a feature of these parts. Today, part of the building houses the museum devoted to one of Albi's most famous sons, the painter Henri de Toulouse-Lautrec. Below the ramparts, on the edge of a cliff that overlooks the River Tarn, is one of the most perfect, and perfectly kept, of all *jardins à la française*. A central circle of box is clipped into patterns, the gaps filled with flowers. It is flanked by shapes of box clipped into rounded sheaf-like patterns, resembling embroidery. Box-edged beds of annuals form boundaries, with smaller circular beds at the base on each side. Running along the palace walls is a bed of pink hydrangeas.

The garden may only be viewed from above, and two long stretches of the walk are shaded by arbours of vines or wisteria. From the northernmost side there are views of the powerfully flowing waters of the river, of bridges and, on the far shore, of a cluster of old houses. The garden is one of the prettiest sights in the whole of France, of jewel-like perfection, a brilliant flight of fancy among the stern buildings of the palace.

Meticulously clipped box and yew compartments filled with bedding plants.

Albi: Parc de Rochegude

Location: S of the city centre

Although this urban park is not well cared for, it still possesses charm. The site is undulating and, for an urban park, very well wooded, with some splendid specimens of individual trees, which include a 250-year-old downy oak (*Quercus pubescens*) and several superb American black walnuts (*Juglans nigra*).

To one side of the house is a beautiful pool and fountain, mounted on stone columns, with lead cherubs spouting water and decoration of medieval character. To one side of the parterre behind the house, four London planes shade a statue of Henry de Paschal de Rochegude (1741–1834), an admiral after whom the garden is named. Behind him, the land falls away to shady groves, winding gravel walks, and a lake – a typical 19th-century park *à l'anglaise*. It is a pity that the town of Albi does not care for all this as much as it deserves – but it is certainly worth a pause for anyone arriving in, or leaving, the town from the south.

Open: Summer, daily, 8am–7pm; winter, daily, 9am–5.30pm

Further information from:
avenue du Maréchal-Foch,
81000 Albi
Tel: 05 63 54 00 20

Nearby sights of interest:
Albi (Musée Toulouse-Lautrec,
Cathédrale de Sainte-Cécile).

 # Arboretum de Balaine

Location: 13km (8 miles) S of Nevers, by the N7

This is one of the oldest arboreta in France, founded in 1805 by Aglaé Adanson, the daughter of Michel Adanson, who had worked in the royal botanic garden attached to the Petit Trianon until 1772. Michel Adanson had also visited gardens in England, and what he saw there must in all probability have influenced his daughter in her plans for the park at Balaine. On this well watered, largely acid site Aglaé Adanson laid out winding walks, bridges across streams, and glades in the woodland to provide suitable microclimates for the more tender plants – necessary, for this is one of the colder parts of France.

This is a garden chiefly for the keen tree lover. In 12ha (30 acres) of land there are over 1,200 species of trees and shrubs. An immense swamp cypress (*Taxodium distichum*) soars into the sky on the banks of the lake behind the house, and there is a grove of gigantic sierra redwoods (*Sequoiadendron giganteum*) nearby. Near the house there is a small nursery which sells some interesting plants.

The house itself is moated and, although you cannot go in, its attractive forecourt is visible from the garden, with rows of lemon trees in fine old glazed *pots d'Anduze*.

Open: Mar to Nov, daily, 9am to 12 noon, 2–7pm

Further information from:
03460 Villeneuve-sur-Allier
Tel: 04 70 43 30 07

The château shrouded in distinguished trees.

Arboretum National des Barres

Location: E of Nogent-sur-Vernisson, 15km (9¼ miles) S of Montargis by the N7

Open: Mid-Mar to mid-Nov, daily, 10am to 12 noon, 2–6pm. Groups by appointment throughout the year

Further information from:
45290 Nogent-sur-Vernisson
Tel: 02 38 97 62 21
Fax: 02 38 97 65 15

The Arboretum des Barres was founded in 1866 by Philippe André de Vilmorin, and today constitutes one of the finest collections of woody plants in Europe. The Vilmorin family, from the 18th century onwards, provided a dynasty of plant collectors and nurserymen who introduced a stream of new plants to Western gardens.

An area of 35ha (86 acres) contains over 8,000 different plants, representing 2,700 different genera, with the emphasis on species. For those wanting to study particular groups, this treasure trove includes 53 species of viburnum, 166 species of rose, 39 species of firs, 58 species of oak, and so on. They are grouped in different ways – the Geographical Collection groups plants according to their countries of origin, the Systematic Collection according to their botanical classification; while the park of the Vilmorin château has a collection of ornamental plants.

 # *La Bastie d'Urfé*

Location: 20km (12½ miles) N of Montbrison, by the D8, the D5 and the D42

Open: 1 Apr to 31 Oct, daily except Tue, 10am to 12 noon, 2.30–5.30pm; 1 Nov to 31 Mar, daily except Tue, 2.30–6pm

Further information from:
42130 Saint-Etienne-le-Molard
Tel: 04 77 97 54 68

In the Renaissance *cour d'honneur*, wrought iron grilles screen a beautiful grotto.

The château at La Bastie d'Urfé, originally a medieval fortified house, was rebuilt in the 1540s by Claude d'Urfé, a diplomat in the service of Henri II. He was posted to Rome and returned to France filled with the excitement of the Renaissance and determined to recreate his estate in the new style. The entrance courtyard is of chaste Renaissance style. A gently rising ramp leads up to an airy first-floor loggia of Italianate character. At the back of the courtyard, stone arches are filled with a delicate iron tracery embellished with vines picked out in gilt. Behind them is one of the most extraordinary and beautiful garden grottoes in France. The room is vaulted, with niches, and all surfaces are exquisitely inlaid with pebble- and shell-work. Some of the imagery derives from classical mythology – a splendid Neptune holds a cargo of shells to his ear and a fishy serpent writhes about his trident – although much of it has never been unravelled.

To one side of the house are the remains of a formal garden of Renaissance character. Eight lawns, edged in box with cones of clipped yew at their corners, are arranged around a simple but elegant summerhouse, supported on pairs of stone columns with Ionic capitals and a curious conical roof. This too dates from the 16th century.

6 *Bordeaux: Jardin Public*

Location: In the centre of the city

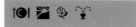

Bordeaux is rich in 18th-century architecture and the layout of the city is contrived to display it to its best advantage. The Jardin Public, started in 1746, was fully integrated into the overall design for the city and the pattern of surrounding streets. Originally formal in design, with elaborate parterres, it was landscaped in the 19th century by the Bordelais landscape architect L-B Fischer. It is to him that we owe the present layout of a long serpentine lake, winding paths, clumps of trees, and elegant arched iron bridges over streams. Good specimens of trees animate the scene, among them a very large Chinese persimmon (*Diospyros kaki*) and a superb *Magnolia grandiflora*.

At the centre of the garden is a herbarium and a botanical library, housed in a neoclassical building. Behind it are the order beds of the Jardin Botanique, in which 2,500 plants are arranged. These include trees, climbers and shrubs, as well as the more usual smaller herbaceous and woody plants. An attractive group of moisture-loving plants is arranged about a pool.

Open: All year, Mon to Sat, 7am to sunset

Further information from:
cours de Verdun, 33000 Bordeaux
Tel: 05 56 90 91 60

Nearby sights of interest:
The city of Bordeaux; vineyards of the Bordelais.

The fine neoclassical botanical library and herbarium.

Manoir Capiplante

Location: In the centre of the village, 4km (2½ miles) N of La Rochelle, by the D104

Open: Easter to Oct,
Mon to Fri, 9am–5pm (closes
Public Holidays)

Further information from:
21 rue Léonce Vieljeu,
17137 Nieul-sur-Mer
Tel: 05 46 37 90 00

Nearby sights of interest:
City of La Rochelle.

The owners of this attractive garden are Les Laboratoires Capiplante, makers of organic cosmetics, which bought the estate in 1988, retaining the house as offices but welcoming visitors to the garden. The house had been built in 1806 but was acquired by Léonce Vieljeu in 1899. Vieljeu became mayor of La Rochelle, and was a member of the Resistance during World War II before being shot in 1944. His son, Pierre, commissioned a garden from the landscape architect Jacques de Wailly, who carried out the work from 1949 to 1950.

The garden lies behind the house, a 20th-century vision of a *jardin à la française*. At the heart of it is a series of formal lawns extending away from the house, with hedges of hornbeam and yew. The lawns are animated with Irish yews, brugmansias clipped into standards, and cones of hornbeam or yew, whose severity is alleviated by beds of blood-red cannas and airy clouds of lavender. At the far end, a square pool is overlooked by a figure of Neptune, trident raised. To one side there is a complete change of mood, with naturalistic plantings of trees and shrubs: Japanese maples, *Clerodendrum trichotomum*, magnolias, dogwoods, and *Metasequoia glyptostroboides*, giving way to open meadows. The scene is enlivened by formal touches – a bench backed by a curving hedge of yew, and a quincunx of silver birches. Walking back towards the house the visitor comes to the Allée aux Lions, at the end of which steps rise to a semicircle of box hedges, presided over by a statue of Apollo on a Baroque plinth.

A 17th-century statue of Apollo against screens of yew and box.

8 *Palais Idéal du Facteur Cheval*

Location: 28km (17¼ miles) N of Romans-sur-Isère, by the D538

Open: Apr to Sep, daily, 9am to 7pm; Oct to Nov, daily, 9.30am–5.30pm; Dec to Jan, daily, 10am–4.30pm (closes 25 Dec and 1 Jan); Feb to Mar, daily, 9.30am–5.30pm

Visitors usually find this remarkable place either irresistibly attractive or profoundly irritating but it is unlikely to leave no impression at all. On his rural round of 32km (20 miles) the postman Cheval, born in 1836, started to dream of making his "ideal palace". One day he noticed a curiously shaped stone by the path, and started a collection of pebbles and shells. At the age of 43, he began to spend all his spare time in the realization of his dream.

No more extraordinary garden building has ever been made, and its peculiarity is sharpened by the ordinariness of the garden. Although there is the odd reference to classical architecture, the building appears to have no overall conception. It is a haphazard accretion of forms that seem to erupt out of the ground like some organic growth. It swarms with decoration, becoming a frenzy of ornament – sometimes abstract patterns but also taking the form of writhing snakes, animals' heads, palm trees, snarling monsters, and figures in niches. Monsieur Cheval worked by moonlight, neglected his family and devoted all his spare time to his obsession. The result has a dream-like intensity and, despite the exuberance of decoration, is marked by an introverted solemnity. It has now become a tourist shrine, with a formidable souk of souvenir sellers jostling at the entrance.

Further information from:
26390 Hauterives
Tel: 04 75 68 81 19
Fax: 04 75 68 88 15

"The ecstasy of a fine dream and the prize of hard work" – surrealism in the garden.

---

9 *Parc Floral de la Court d'Aron*

Location: 37km (23 miles) E of Les Sables-d'Olonne by D949

Open: 29 Mar to 28 Sep, daily, 10am–7pm
Open: Jul to Aug, daily, 10am–12.30pm, 2–6.30pm

There is nothing like this in France, or anywhere else that I know of. It is essentially a display garden where gardeners can see how the mild climate of these parts may be used to cultivate tender and unusual plants in a variety of successful combinations. A 5m-high (16ft) banana zips above an Irish yew, intermingling its giant leaves with the delicate fronds of *Albizzia julibrissin*. The velvety scarlet flowers of *Lobelia cardinalis* glow among the sombre leaves of one of the purple cultivars of *Cotinus coggygria*.

There is a great deal of water in the garden, used to full effect, so that groves of mopheaded *Cyperus papyrus* look as at home as in some Egyptian wadi. A most spectacular sight in high

Further information from:
65540 Saint-Cyr-en-Talmondais
Tel: 02 51 30 86 74
Fax: 02 51 30 87 37

summer is a lake, where the surface quivers with sheets of the sacred lotus (*Nelumbo nucifera*). Away from the water, paths lead into woodland where there are all sorts of different plantings – a meadow garden of blue and violet plants, and a large collection of dahlia cultivars. There are good ideas for planting here, such as the excellent combination of lemon kniphofia, purple fennel, and cordyline. Gardeners will find much to look at and admire.

Open: Apr to May, daily, 10am–12.30pm, 2–7pm; Jun to Sep, daily, 9.30am–7pm; Oct to Mar, 10am–12.30pm, 2pm to sunset. Guided visits only. Also by appointment

Further information from:
24590 Salignac
Tel: 05 53 28 99 71
Fax: 05 53 30 39 89

10   *Manoir d'Eyrignac*

Location: 13km (8 miles) NE of Sarlat by minor roads

Hidden in rural countryside, the Manoir d'Eyrignac is a pretty 17th-century manor house. The garden is an elaborate formal arrangement, which supposedly dates from the 18th century but was comprehensively recreated in the 1960s.

The entrance to the garden lies at the end of a long drive, where the house looks out over a shallow valley. Elaborate topiary and hedging frames a sequence of rooms and passages which lead to the house, and a long walk has curving buttresses of hornbeam interspersed with dumpy columns of yew. A rondel of hornbeam hedges has windows cut into its walls and a star-shaped pattern of cobbles at the centre. Near the house, a stylized *parterre à la française* has sweeping curves of clipped box and soaring Italian cypresses. Beyond it, a long pool is edged with domes of clipped box in Tuscan pots.

The garden provides a feast of ornament and is full of lively reinterpretations of the language of formal gardening. Maintained to perfectionist standards, it does, however, teeter on the verge of preciosity, having something of the air of a shrine – as though it should be spoken of only in a hushed voice.

Columns of yew and curves of hornbeam create a dazzling geometry of formality.

Gaillac: Parc de Foucaud

Location: 22km (13½ miles) W of Albi, by the N88, in the centre of the town

Open: All year, daily, 7am–7pm

Further information from:
avenue Dom Vaysette,
81600 Gaillac
Tel: 05 63 57 18 25
Fax: 05 63 57 33 45

Nearby sights of interest:
Albi (Cathédrale de Sainte-Cécile, Musée Toulouse-Lautrec); Toulouse (old city, Basilique de Saint-Sernin, Musée des Augustins).

Gaillac is an agreeable small town at the centre of wine-growing country, where good sparkling and red wines are made. The Château de Foucaud is a 17th-century house built of the characteristic pale, pink-brown bricks – the universal building material around here. The garden at first seems to be a fairly undistinguished public park of no special interest and the façade of the house on this side is crisply austere. However, on the other side of the house a completely different mood prevails. An elaborate double staircase leads down from an ornamental doorway on the *piano nobile* to a terraced garden below. A square parterre has a circular pool and a fountain, with drums of clipped euonymus and box, and beds of annuals. In one corner is a beautiful summerhouse, with bold pillars at each corner and a tiled roof of a sweeping ogee shape. Curious terracotta fish-tailed men besport themselves on the cornice. Although the interior has been vandalized, it still has traces of a most decorative room, with elaborate vaulted niches crowned with plaster shells in each corner.

To one side of the summerhouse, and at a slightly lower level, is a scalloped pond edged with stone moulding, and an island planted with an extraordinary sheaf of bamboos at least 8m (26ft) high. The garden is irrigated with an elaborate water system originating from an ornamental pool at the bottom of the staircase, and then chanelled into two semicircular pools with grotesque masks, and thence down either side of the parterre in narrow rills. All this has a fine flavour of southern exuberance, hidden away from the rather prim façade which faces the public on the other side. The château has been impeccably restored and houses a museum of local artists and of local history.

The 17th-century summerhouse, like a miniature castle keep.

113

Open: Apr to Sep, daily, 9am–8pm; Oct to Mar, daily, 9.30am–6.30pm

Further information from:
44190 Gétigné Clisson
Tel: 02 40 54 75 85
Fax: 02 40 03 99 22

Nearby sights of interest:
Nantes (château, Musée des Beaux Arts).

The Temple of Vesta on the rocky cliffs above the River Sèvre.

12 *Domaine de la Garenne Lemot*

Location: 30km (18½ miles) SE of Nantes, SE of the town of Clisson

Few gardens in France display the full-blown picturesque style so emphatically as La Garenne Lemot and few are so bound up in historical events. The nearby town of Clisson was all but destroyed in 1793 during the anti-Republican war. Frédéric Lemot, a sculptor who had worked in Rome and been seduced by the beauties of the Campagna, fell in love with the Sèvre Valley and at the beginning of the 19th century bought a piece of woodland on its banks. He, in collaboration with other like-minded artists and architects, rebuilt Clisson, giving free rein to a love of Italian scenery – to this day the town preserves an extraordinarily Italianate character.

Lemot built a house at La Garenne and laid out a striking garden which has since been restored. The essence of the site is best understood from the semicircular viewing terrace behind the house. The land falls away abruptly at this point, its rocky slopes leading down to the river below. To the right, on the far banks, the remains of the medieval castle are seen with the tiled roofs of the rebuilt Clisson beyond. Facing the terrace on the wooded slopes on the far side is a classical Temple of Friendship, where Lemot was buried in 1827. This mixture of lofty classical architecture and wooded crags is the very spirit of the picturesque.

The visitor should now turn back past the house and go towards the Rondpoint de Diane from which a path leads towards the river. On its very edge is the Temple of Vesta – inspired by the Roman original at Tivoli – a colonnaded circular building below which a cascade of rocks tumbles down to the water. Energetic visitors will continue down to the riverside where peaceful walks pass under a canopy of trees. Here is a selection of more monuments, including an Ancient Tomb with the inscription *Et in Arcadia Ego*, and Rousseau's Rock celebrating the writer whose ideas inspired this style of gardening – especially the notion of the solitary dream-filled walk among the beauties of nature, gently animated by the hand of man.

Château de Hautefort

Location: 45km (28 miles) E of Périgueux, by the D5

The sight of Hautefort from the distance is unforgettable –
rearing up above a little hill village, with the plain spread out
below. The château has its origins in the Middle Ages but the
present building dates largely from the 17th century. The estate
was acquired in 1929 by Baron Henry de Bastard, to whom we
owe its restoration and the creation of the formal gardens.

A winding path takes the visitor up to the castle ramparts,
with the gardens hugging the walls. Formality rules here, with
hedges and topiary of box and yew, whose bold simple shapes
and lively patterns make a fine foil for the castle fortifications.
Just before the bridge that leads to the castle is a splendid pair
of modern parterres in triangular patterns, with long shapes of
contrasting silver and common box executed with tremendous
panache. A monumental parterre of broad box hedges, devoid
of flowers, makes a spectacular entrance in the first courtyard.

Patterns of parterres girdle the castle walls, with the spaces
between the hedges filled with bedding plants in blocks
of a single colour or well-judged combinations. One has
interlacing box hedges clipped at different heights, with topiary
cones and mounds – some in silver variegated box. When I was
last there, some of the compartments were strikingly filled with
dwarfcannas with lemon-yellow flowers. As the visitor circles
the castle, mesmerizing views of the surrounding countryside
compete for attention.

Open: Palm Sunday to Oct,
9am to 12 noon, 2–7pm
Open: As above

Further information from:
24390 Hautefort
Tel: 05 53 50 59 46
Fax: 05 53 50 55 03

20th-century evocations of
classical parterres embellish
the 17th-century château.

Open: All year, daily, sunrise to sunset

Further information from:
87340 La Jonchère-Saint-Maurice
Tel: 05 55 34 53 13

A secret lake lies at the heart of the arboretum.

Arboretum de la Jonchère

Location: 28km (17¼ miles) NE of Limoges, by the N20 and the D914

This arboretum, which specializes in conifers, is for passionate tree-lovers only. It is not far from Mont-Méry (see p.120), and may be taken in on the same visit. Originally a nursery, started in 1885 by Henri Gerardin, it was landscaped by André Laurent but later abandoned. It subsequently became an arboretum, passing into the hands of the Office National de Forêts. The relatively high rainfall and hot summers here promote swift growth.

One of its particular charms is that it has the air of a piece of natural woodland – there is no "specimen planting". Plants are well labelled, but many are tucked away in odd corners, so the more you look the more you see. Inconspicuous paths lead uphill, and the visitor is quickly rewarded by a magnificent grove of coast redwoods (*Sequoia sempervirens*). Some of these specimens date from Gerardin's time, as does a magnificent western hemlock (*Tsuga heterophylla*). This was planted in 1890 and has now assumed a majestic size, resembling a giant Christmas tree. A lovely old Japanese umbrella pine (*Sciadopitys verticillata*) has an extraordinary gnarled trunk. On a warm summer's day this coniferous jungle, perfumed with resin, is a memorable place for a long and informative walk, with much to marvel at.

Open: All year, daily, 8am to sunset

Further information from:
place de la Cathédrale,
87031 Limoges Cédex
Tel: 05 55 45 62 67
Fax: 05 55 45 64 37

Nearby sights of interest:
Musée de Porcelaines.

Limoges: Jardin de l'Evêché and Jardin Botanique

Location: In the centre of city, next to the cathedral

There are two gardens here on neighbouring sites: the Jardin de l'Evêché, a formal garden laid out before the former bishop's palace, and immediately alongside it a botanic garden. The palace – now a museum containing superb Limoges enamels and porcelain – is a distinguished 18th-century building. Below its south façade, a terrace has a double parterre of shaped lawns, edged with fortissimo beds of annuals. These are freely planted, with tall cleomes and fuchsias creating bushy shapes above smaller plants. At the end is a bastion overlooking a lower terrace, ornamented with curving patterns of close-clipped grass.

To one side of this is the Jardin Botanique, of which the first part, of order beds, has an attractive position below the buttresses of the south side of the cathedral nave. At a lower level is a thematic collection of plants grouped according to particular categories: poisonous plants, useful plants, medicinal plants, and so on. This part of the garden is laid out formally, with a broad central walk of rectangular pools flanked by rows of obelisks of clipped yews, and the plants disposed in symmetrical rows of beds on either side. The final part of the Jardin Botanique, devoted to plants indigenous to the Limousin area, is planted naturalistically with winding walks. The whole garden is finely cared for and makes an admirable place to visit.

16 Luçon: Jardin Dumaine

Location: 49km (30 miles) E of Les-Sables-d'Olonne, by the D949, in the centre of the town, near the town hall

Open: All year, daily, 8am–7pm

Further information from:
3 rue de l'Hôtel de Ville,
85400 Luçon
Tel: 02 51 56 36 52
Fax: 02 51 56 03 56

Luçon is a sleepy little town with an exceptionally lively public garden. At the entrance, there are splendid displays of carpet bedding – a bust of Henri Dumaine on a plinth emerges from a mounded bed with virtuoso swirling patterns of sedums, and a froth of red impatiens. In the first part of the garden proper, a lily pond has a magnificent fountain with nymphs and cherubs supporting a basin, while frogs spout water at them from the pool below. The pool is edged with palm trees in *caisses de Versailles*, and beautiful ultramarine glazed urns on plinths are filled with pelargoniums. An airy cast iron bandstand is crowned with a filigree lantern, and bedding schemes about its base harmonize with the cheerful spirit of the architecture.

At the centre of the park in cool woodland is a lake from which erupts a spectacular single jet of water, with a grotto on one side. Beyond this, on a brilliant green Grande Pelouse, are some extraordinary garden ornaments. A giraffe, made of *Helichrysum petiolare*, rears up from a pool of red impatiens, startled by a many-branched cactus at its feet. A tableau of one of La Fontaine's fables – the Fox and the Grapes – is intricately worked in many different plants. In other places, a prancing horse leaps in the air, and a wild boar snouts in the undergrowth. It is all carried off with irresistible panache – the sort of thing which, almost, gives kitsch a good name. On the way out do not miss the curious remains of a *théâtre de verdure* that seems to have strayed into the garden from an earlier time. The whole garden is beautifully cared for, to the delight of the citizens of Luçon.

An airy, filigree bandstand and light-hearted borders.

Lyon: Parc de la Tête d'Or

Location: NE in the city centre

Open: Apr to Sep, daily, 6am–11pm; Oct to Mar, daily, 6am–9pm. Jardin Botanique: 7.30–11.30am and 1–6pm in summer; 8–11.30am and 1–5pm in winter

Further information from:
place Leclerc, 69459 Lyon Cédex
Tel: 04 78 89 53 52
Fax: 04 78 89 15 90

Nearby sights of interest:
The old city of Lyon; Musée des Tissus.

Hard by the banks of the Rhône, the Parc de la Tête d'Or is thoroughly worthy of one of the most fascinating and attractive cities in France. Covering an area of well over 100ha (247 acres), it is not only a distinguished piece of landscaping but, for gardeners, packed with interest. It was laid out in 1856 by the brothers Denis and Eugène Bühler, who created an immense serpentine lake fed by the waters of the Rhône. The rich alluvial soil has allowed trees, in particular, to flourish magnificently. The Bühlers paid careful attention to their grouping, which gives the park much of its beauty. The site is largely flat, apart from the artificial declivity of the lake, so the planting of trees of different heights and character was the best way of animating the surface. Walks wind under trees, with many benches, and in the great heat of summer it is immensely popular with the Lyonnais.

Of further particular interest is the outstanding Jardin Botanique. This was first established elsewhere in 1793, but moved to the Parc de la Tête d'Or when it was founded. It has a vast collection of plants, with 8,000 hardy plants and over 5,000 tropical plants cultivated under glass. Specialists will relish the tropical plants as there are several major collections, including bromeliads, cacti, epiphytes, ferns, and orchids. There are also collections of exceptional interest to gardeners among the hardy plants: a fruticetum contains 350 varieties of fruit trees; there are 300 cultivars of peony; and an excellent alpine garden with a fine range of plants. Of particular local interest is the range of roses. France in the 19th century led the world in rose breeding, and Lyon was at the heart of it. Around 130 species roses provides a fascinating display of the raw material available to breeders, and the beds of old cultivars, with over 350 varieties, are enthralling. Lyon was a city of pioneering nurserymen and many of the roses displayed had their origins here. The famous firm of Pernet-Ducher, founded in 1881, a hybrid of two old rose-breeding families, introduced, among many roses, 'Cécile Brünner' and 'Madame Caroline Testout'. These are some of the subjects of special interest, but La Tête d'Or is also well provided with the skilful ornamental planting and decorative exuberance found in other French public parks.

A 19th-century sculpture of a centaur garnished with impeccable carpet bedding.

Château de Malle

Location: 3km (2 miles) NW of Langon, by minor roads

Many of the châteaux of the Bordelais are architecturally of little interest. Malle is an exception, a dazzling early 17th-century house of pale stone, with carved detail, and flanked by a pair of pepperpot towers. The entrance to the garden is through the house: straight into a hall and out the other side into the garden.

A central walk leads between lawns to steps, and from there to a long grassy terrace running parallel to the château. All along its length are full-length stone figures mounted on tall plinths. At one end of the terrace, a three-part loggia is ornamented with grotesque masks and figures from the Commedia dell'Arte. At the other end of the terrace, there is a balustrade and views of the vineyards. Behind the terrace, a shady grove with a central walk aligned on the centre of the house and decorated with urns on pedestals, ends in a pretty *trompe l'oeil* door in the wall. The whole garden was made in the 18th century, and a contemporary plan shows the layout, with rather sharper edges, looking exactly as it is today.

Malle makes delicious *cru classé* Sauternes and fine red Graves, both of which may be bought at the château. Vineyards with yellow roses flowering along their edge may be seen on the way back to the car park. These roses are frequently seen in Bordelais vineyards, acting as an early warning system for mildew – roses catch it more quickly than vines.

Open: Apr to Oct, daily, 10am to 12 noon, 2–6.30pm

Further information from:
33210 Preignac
Tel: 05 56 62 36 86
Fax: 05 56 76 82 40

Nearby sights of interest:
Bordeaux (old city, Musée des Beaux Arts); vineyards of the Bordelais.

Seen from above, the garden layout has classical harmony of detail.

 ## Château de Merville

Location: In Merville, 20km (12½ miles) NW of Toulouse, by the D2 and minor roads

This beautiful and very unusual estate has recently undergone restoration and offers visitors a rare chance to see a house and garden unlike any other. Merville is an ancient place, so that the present château, built between 1743 and 1759, is relatively recent. This grand provincial house of great charm was built for the Marquis de Chalvet-Rochemonteix, to his own designs. His descendants, the Beaumont du Repaire family, still live there. The garden was laid out at the same time and, again, it is to the Marquis that we owe the design.

The Marquis was inspired by French formal gardens of the previous century and he created a formal woodland garden, with an elaborate pattern of box-hedged paths with groves of oaks behind. *Allées* thread their way through the woods, building up an elaborate pattern, some leading nowhere and others to a *salle*

Open: Easter to Oct, Sun, Mon, Public Holidays and Ascension Day, 2–7pm. Groups (15 or more) all year round by appointment
Open: As above

Further information from:
31330 Merville
Tel: 05 61 85 67 46
Fax: 05 62 13 77 21

Nearby sights of interest:
Toulouse (Basilique Saint-Sernin, Musée des Augustins).

de verdure (*the Salle de Bal*) or to the Grand Rond Point. The latter is a huge circular lawn, slightly concave, with a pool at its centre. On either side of it, steps lead up to a broad grass walk, flanked on one side by a superb pair of stone pines (*Pinus pinea*).

Merville is not for lovers of flowers; but as a formal garden of hedges, grass, and trees, it is both austere and beautiful.

20 *Parc de Mont-Méry*

Open: 15 Mar to 15 Nov, Sun and Public Holidays, 2–6pm; Jun also open Sat, 10am–6pm

Further information from:
87240 Ambazac
Tel: 05 55 56 60 01

Nearby sights of interest:
Limoges (Musée A. Dubouché).

An American house, with trees from the American continent, in a French setting.

Location: 30km (18½ miles) NE of Limoges, by the N20 and the D914, on the edge of the village of Ambazac

The estate of Mont-Méry was the creation of Theodore Haviland, whose father, David, emigrated from America in 1842, coming to Limoges to found the porcelain factory that remains one of the most prominent producers of fine French china. He commissioned a house from the grandest New York architects of the day, McKim, Mead & White, with a setting to match, laid out by the greatest of American landscape architects, Frederick Law Olmsted, the creator of New York's Central Park. Although Mont-Méry survives today in a more or less dishevelled state, it is, nevertheless, one of the finest 19th-century landscapes in France, and one of the most unforgettable.

The house is richly eclectic in style, and decorated with all sorts of fine details, including bright turquoise ceramic tiles in a loggia, and a series of carved stone capitals showing the process of china making. High on an eminence, it looks down on the park below – to one side of the house is a viewing terrace shaded by beautiful silver limes (*Tilia tomentosa*). Everywhere in the park are fine American plants: scatterings of the flowering dogwood *Cornus florida* by the *rivière anglaise* in the lower parkland; a vast *Magnolia macrophylla* north of the house; the calico bush (*Kalmia latifolia*) in many places; and superb specimens of *Sequoiadendron giganteum*. Throughout the park there are intriguing decorative details: leading up to the house is an *allée* of old *Pieris formosa* and rhododendrons, their branches bending over to form a tunnel; finally, at the entrance to the park, is a formal chicken-house with a pediment, in front of which is a circular pool and fountain.

The detailed history of Mont-Méry is yet to be written. Here, in the rolling country of the Limousin, is a New England estate garden cast up, magnificently, on foreign shores.

Château de Pizay

Location: 16km (10 miles) N of Villefranche-sur-Saône, by the N6

The intensively planted patchwork of the vineyards of the Beaujolais fill a huge plain between Villefranche and Mâcon. Pizay is in the southern part of this area, very near the village of Beaujeu from which the wine derives its name. There was a formal garden at Pizay in the 17th century, but the garden today depends upon a single, quite recent feature: enchanting topiary of yew – dumpy cones surmounted by a series of concentric circles of diminishing size. They are visible from afar across the flat land. Pizay is a wine-growing estate and, furthermore, a hotel and restaurant. You may buy admirable cru Beaujolais here – Morgon – after you have sauntered among the yew shapes.

Open: All year, daily, 9am–6pm

Further information from:
69220 Saint-Jean-d'Ardières
Tel: 04 74 66 26 10
Fax: 04 74 69 60 66

Nearby sights of interest:
Vineyards of Beaujolais and Maconnais; Bourg-en-Bresse (Eglise de Brou).

Château de la Roche-Courbon

Location: 20km (12½ miles) NW of Saintes, by the N137

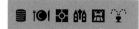

The château, with its two massive pepperpot towers, dates from the late 15th century, although it was substantially remodelled in the 17th century. In the ownership of the Courbon family, the estate had a glittering history until it passed by marriage in the late 18th century to the Comte d'Hédouville, whose creditors forced him to sell it in 1817. The château remained uninhabited and became an object of romantic fascination to the writer Pierre Loti, who was born nearby at Rochefort: "I travelled the world but the locked-up château and its fathomless groves of oaks haunted my imagination." Loti publicized the plight of the estate, which was eventually bought in 1920 by his friend, the industrialist Pierre Chénereau. By that time the valley of the River Bruant below the house, where in the 17th century there had been an elaborate formal garden, had become a marshy swamp and the original garden had all but disappeared. Between 1925 and 1935 the landscape architect Ferdinand Duprat recreated a formal garden freely based on 17th-century ideas.

Below the south side of the château are simple parterres of lawns, gravel paths of contrasting colour, and topiary of box and yew. Beyond, a huge T-shaped pool points towards an ornate grotto and cascade, flanked by grandiose stairs which ascend the steep hill with woodland on either side. From the top of

Open: All year, daily, 9am to 12 noon, 2–6.30pm (closes 5.30pm in winter); (closes 25 Dec and 1 Jan)
Open: 16 Jun to 4 Sep, daily, 10am to 12 noon, 2.30–6.30pm; 15 Sep to 15 Jun, daily except Thu, 10am to 12 noon, 2.30–6.30pm

Further information from:
17250 Saint-Porchaire
Tel: 05 46 95 60 10
Fax: 05 46 95 65 22

A recreated 17th-century garden with 20th-century planting.

these steps, the formal pool is seen at its best: a *miroir d'eau* reflecting the façade of the château. Follow signs to the *grottes*, on the way out, and walk a considerable distance through attractive woodland. This will eventually lead to some natural-looking caves which are certainly picturesque but do not appear ever to have been part of the designed landscape. Do not miss a visit to the château; its magnificent 17th-century interiors give a vivid idea of the estate in its heyday.

Open: All the time

Further information from:
17300 Rochefort
Tel and Fax: 05 46 87 59 84

23 *Rochefort: Corderie Royale*

Location: In the centre of the old town of Rochefort

Strictly speaking, the Jardin des Retours is not a garden at all; rather it is a landscaped setting for the many marvellous restored buildings of Louis XIV's naval yard, and celebrates the happy return of sailors and of plant-hunters bringing new treasures home. The yard was built in the 1660s on a virgin site on the banks of the River Charente, quite near its estuary. In recent years the remaining 17th-century buildings have been restored and turned to various cultural purposes which include Le Centre International de la Mer and a splendid recreated rope factory installed in the original building of the Corderie Royale.

Along the marshy banks of the river, a path is embellished with naturalistic planting – alders, ash, grasses and sedges, Guelder rose (*Viburnum opulus*), hazel, and willows. Half-concealed in these groves is the reconstructed deck of a ship with a demonstration of rigging. At the far end of the immensely long, low building of the rope factory, a charming yew maze, the Labyrinthe des Batailles Navales, celebrates naval battles of the past. A glasshouse with a collection of begonias honours the memory of the man after whom they were named, Michel Bégon, 17th-century Governor of French Canada and patron of botany. He and his grandson, the Marquis de la Galissonière, were responsible for bringing back to France many North American plants, some of which have been planted in the Jardin de la Marine in their memory – among them tulip trees (*Liriodendron tulipifera*), magnolias, and possum-wood (*Diospyros virginiana*). All this seems an admirable way of bringing life to what could have been a frigid exercise in industrial archaeology.

The beautiful 17th-century rope-works and a stately lime *allée*.

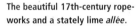

Tarbes: Jardin Massey

Location: On the northern edge of the old town

A prosperous citizen of Tarbes, Placide Massey, left this estate and almost all his fortune to the city. It is now a fine public park with much to interest the visitor. Avenues of tulip trees (*Liriodendron tulipifera*) and of Chusan palms (*Trachycarpus fortunei*) give exotic structure to the garden, and many good specimens of trees are to be found, among them a magnificent *Liquidambar styraciflua* and superb cedars of Lebanon. The more interesting specimens are clearly labelled with not only their scientific and French names but also their names in Provençal.

A domed orangery of glass and ornate metalwork houses a collection of epiphytic orchids, tree ferns, cacti, palms, and other tender plants. Among the cacti is a magnificent old *Dasylirion longissimum*, now 50 years old, looking like a giant pine-cone with a bush of slender shoots. In the garden, there is a display of the grape varieties used to make the delicious local red wine, Madiran. Here are Cabernet Sauvignon and Cabernet Franc but also the much less common local varieties such as Fer Servadou, Petit-courbu, and Tannat. With its winding sandy paths, and decorative snaking rills of water, the Jardin Massey is a delicious retreat on a hot summer's day.

Open: Oct to Mar, daily, 8am–6pm; Apr to 14 Jun, daily, 8am–8pm; 15 Jun to 15 Aug, daily, 7am–9pm; 16 Aug to Sep, daily, 8am–8pm

Further information from:
place Henri Bordes, 65000 Tarbes
Tel: 05 62 93 11 74

Nearby sights of interest:
The Pyrenees.

A statue of St Christopher erupts from thickets of juniper and thuja.

Key to gardens

1	Aix-en-Provence: Pavillon de Vendôme	9	Nîmes: Jardin de la Fontaine
2	Jardin d'Albertas	10	Bambouseraie de Prafrance
3	Hyères: Parc St Bernard	11	Villa Ephrussi de Rothschild
4	Jardin Alpin du Lautaret	12	Villa Thuret
5	Marseille: Parc Borély	13	Villa Val Rahmeh
6	Menton: Clos du Peyronnet		
7	Château de la Mignarde		
8	Monaco: Jardin Exotique		

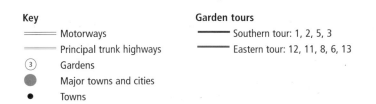

Key

- ═══ Motorways
- ═══ Principal trunk highways
- ③ Gardens
- ⬤ Major towns and cities
- • Towns

Garden tours

- ▬▬ Southern tour: 1, 2, 5, 3
- ▬▬ Eastern tour: 12, 11, 8, 6, 13

South-eastern France

PARC NATIONAL
DE MERCANTOUR
N202

13
6
8
Menton
Monaco
11
NICE
12
Cap d'Antibes
CANNES

Tropez

Were it not for the mild, warm climate and the lure of the Mediterranean, there would be no good gardens here. The land is poor and the landscape, though beautiful, lends itself to gardening only with difficulty. There have never been any great estates here, and the provincial gentry rarely spent money on their gardens. Although there are some attractive historic gardens, of a kind found nowhere else in France, it is the more recent gardens that provide most of the horticultural interest.

In the 19th century the Côte d'Azur was taken up by the rich and fashionable and gradually became one of the world's playgrounds. The gardening possibilities were soon realized. The American writer Edith Wharton made an outstanding garden at the Château-Sainte-Claire, above Hyères. She was enraptured by the place and refers to the "unbelievable profusion" of the plants and "the thrill of the adventure". This love affair with the Côte d'Azur

The rose garden at the Parc Borély at Marseille.

125

brought countless gardeners to its shores. Many of the best gardens that exist today are those of the former private estates which are now in institutional ownership, such as the Villa Val Rahmeh (see p.140).

In Provence, several gardens go back to the more distant past. At Nîmes the beautiful Jardin de la Fontaine (see p.134), laid out in the 18th century, has Roman antecedents. The Pavillon Vendôme at Aix-en-Provence (see p.128) is set in a formal garden dating from the same period. The Jardin d'Albertas and the Château de la Mignarde, both of the 18th century, preserve gardens which vividly reflect elegant provincial life of that time.

The gardens of the Côte d'Azur have three particular attractions to visitors: the beauty of their setting and layout; the glimpses of an exotic way of life; and the extraordinarily wide range of plants grown. The Villa Ephrussi de Rothschild (see pp.136–9) vividly displays two of these attractions. The Clos du Peyronnet (see p.131) combines charm of setting, botanical excitement, and distinguished garden design. Some of these gardens provide a unique opportunity to study plants that are grown nowhere else in France and in very few places elsewhere in Europe. The Villa Thuret (see p.140) displays a jungle of exotic rarities and Monaco's Jardin Exotique (see p.133) is a prickly paradise for cactus lovers.

Away from the coast are two plant collections which also take advantage of the climate. The Bambouseraie de Prafrance at Anduze (see p.135) has a unique range of bamboos. The alpine garden at Le Lautaret (see p.130) has one of the finest settings of any garden in the world among the peaks of the Hautes-Alpes.

The gardens in this region present great diversity in a relatively small area. Many of them display a warm exuberance which is intoxicating. In winter a spell of balmy weather can bring out a surprising number of flowers.

Dramatic shapes of old succulents at the Jardin Exotique in Monaco.

🍽 ‖‖

🏠 **Open:** All year, daily, 9am
to 12 noon, 2–7pm

Further information from:
13 rue de la Molle,
13100 Aix-en-Provence
Tel: 04 42 21 05 78
Fax: 04 42 23 57 75

Nearby sights of interest:
Marseille (Basilique Notre-Dame-
de-la-Garde, Vieux Port, Musée
Grobet-Labadié).

🍁 1 *Aix-en-Provence:*
Pavillon de Vendôme

Location: In the centre of the city, W of the cathedral

The Pavillon de Vendôme is an exquisite 17th- and 18th-century town house, set in formal gardens that perfectly match the atmosphere of the house. The house, of honey-coloured stone, was built in 1665 to the designs of Antoine Matisse for the Duc de Vendôme – who was also a Cardinal – as a discreet place in which to entertain his mistress, Madame de Rascas. Its simple classical restraint explodes into eccentricity with a pair of giant caryatids supporting the porch over the front door – their faces frowning with the burden. Originally built on a single storey, two further floors were added in the 18th century.

The garden, whose essential layout is of the same date as the house, is divided into four lawns with a cruciform pattern of gravel paths and a central pool and fountain. The paths are lined with topiary of box and yew. At the end of the central path leading from the front door there are fine urns and a water-trough, half concealed in trees and shrubs. The house itself is flanked by a pair of elegant pavilions, which are also partly hidden. The garden entrance has handsome steps and wrought iron gates with piers capped with urns. The whole garden is concealed behind walls, lined with trees and shrubs, making a delicious shady oasis in the heat of a provençal afternoon. Its air of intimacy remains intact, eloquently reminding visitors of its original purpose.

The dazzlingly decorative façade of the pavilion.

⬢ 🔷

 Open: Jun to Aug, daily,
3–7pm; May, Sep and Oct, Sat,
Sun and Public Holidays, 2–6pm.
Groups by appointment at other
times

Further information from:
RN 8, 13320 Bouc-Bel-Air
Tel: 04 42 22 29 77
or 04 42 24 01 35
Fax: 04 42 22 94 71

Nearby sights of interest:
Marseille (Basilique Notre-Dame-
de-la-Garde, Vieux Port, Musée
Grobet-Labadié).

🍁 2 *Jardin d'Albertas*

Location: 11km (7 miles) S of Aix-en-Provence, on the N8

Albertas is an alluring fragment of a garden, created in the 18th century for a château that was never built. The estate is bisected by the busy main road from Marseille to Aix-en-Provence. It is a formal garden, sculpted into bold terraces of turf, and richly ornamented with statues and stonework. Water is a major feature here, and at the head of the drive is a horseshoe-shaped pool and *buffet d'eau*, backed by a canal in the shade of plane trees. Behind it lies a pool with pilasters around it in the form of caryatids, above which tritons trumpet water. A path leads between the beds of a parterre towards an opening in the woods guarded by griffons. Here is a grove with a headless statue lurking in the shade. Despite the busy road, the place seems untouched by modern times and preserves an aura of Italianate melancholy.

Hyères: Parc St Bernard

Location: 20km (12½ miles) E of Toulon by N98, on the hill above Hyères

Charles and Marie-Laure de Noailles were great patrons of the arts, with a taste for the avant garde; Charles, in addition, was a passionate and immensely knowledgeable gardener. On a hilly site above Hyères they commissioned a modernistic villa, in 1924, from the architect Robert Mallet-Stevens. A little later, they asked the architect and garden designer Gabriel Guevrekian to design a garden to be attached to the villa. He designed an isosceles triangle pointing away from the end of the villa and laid out in a firmly geometric way, with squares of tulips, a little rectangular pool, and brightly-coloured mosaics. In recent years the villa has been restored and Guevrekian's garden reconstructed. It is not a garden in which to walk – it may be admired from the windows of the villa or by peering over the flanking wall. Although it may give something of the flavour of modernism, the reconstruction has not been executed precisely according to the original plan, which has far greater subtlety.

Some visitors may much prefer the flower-covered terraces that lie below the villa. Here is a profusion of old olive trees, *Pinus pinaster*, huge mounds of sweetly-scented cherry pie (*Heliotropium arborescens*), the lovely jagged leaves of *Melianthus major*, and the exotic sprawling flower stems of *Beschorneria yuccoides*, jutting out over the terraces. Although this part of the Côte d'Azur is now horribly built up, the view of the Mediterranean through the rich and ornamental planting gives a vivid idea of the magic that first drew people to its shores.

Open: All year, daily, 8am–6pm

Further information from: 83400 Hyères

Nearby sights of interest: Marseille (Basilique de Notre-Dame-de-la-Garde, Vieux Port, Musée Grobet-Labadié, Musée d'Archéologie Méditerranéenne).

The reconstruction of Gabriel Guevrekian's startling avant garde garden.

Jardin Alpin du Lautaret

Location: 30km (18½ miles) NW of Briançon, by the N91

Open: From the last Sun in Jun to the first Sun in Sep, daily, 10am–6.30pm

Further information from:
col du Lautaret,
05220 Monetier-les-Bains
Tel: 04 76 51 46 00
or 04 76 51 49 40
Fax: 04 76 51 44 63

Nearby sights of interest:
Magnificent scenery of the Hautes-Alpes.

An alpine garden in a true alpine setting is a great rarity. Here, at over 2,000m (6,562ft), in spectacular alpine scenery, is a feast for lovers of alpine plants. Winters are cold, with an average minimum temperature in January of –9°C (16°F), and bitter winds lash the slopes. Nonetheless, the brief summer months produce bursts of flowering and provide the opportunity of seeing a unique collection in a beautiful setting. Surrounded by meadows, winding paths lead round beds and pools, with plants grouped according to their countries of origin – flora of most of the world's mountainous regions are represented. There are collections of particular families (Caryophyllaceae, Compositae, and Rosaceae), of grasses, of herbaceous perennials, of bulbs, and of the few trees that will grow in such extreme conditions. Free refreshment is offered – water from the nearby glacier.

Marseille: Parc Borély

Location: Towards the S of central Marseille

Open: All year, daily, 7am–10pm

Further information from:
allée Borély, 13008 Marseille
Tel: 04 91 55 14 68

Nearby sights of interest:
Marseille (Basilique de Notre-Dame-de-la-Garde, Vieux Port, Musée Grobet-Labadié).

J-M Folon's delightful bronze fountain-figure.

This is a busy public garden occupying a splendid position, with the Mediterranean in front and jagged outlines of the mountains behind. Louis Borély was a shipowner who built the château here in 1767, although it has subsequently been much altered. In front of it, in keeping with its formality, is a *jardin à la française*, with avenues of mopheaded limes. The best part of the park is that designed in informal style in the 19th century by Jacques Barillet-Deschamps. Here, there are many good trees, some of them rare, such as the Chinese nutmeg tree, *Torreya grandis*, of which there are several beautiful examples. Fine specimens of less unusual species include planes, in particular *Platanus orientalis* and a superb *P.* x *hispanica*, which have grown into magnificent trees. An exuberant rose garden – almost entirely of modern cultivars – is very decorative, with the plants trained as standards or festooning tunnels and arches. A grotto and pool made in 1860, with a rocky cascade with moss and ferns, is embellished with a charming fountain by the artist J-M Folon. A solemn bronze figure stands on an island with one arm outstretched and a bird balanced on its palm, from which water gushes.

Menton: Clos du Peyronnet

Location: On the E side of Menton

The Clos du Peyronnet has an enviable position on slopes above the bay of Garavan, close to the Italian border. Derick and Barbara Waterfield first came here in 1915, and it was their son Humphrey who gave the garden its strong formal lines and distinguished planting. The present owner, William Waterfield, Humphrey's nephew, has brought to the garden his passion for rare bulbs.

Before the Waterfields came, the garden had been terraced for the cultivation of lemons and olives, and this underlying shaping of the land is still plainly visible. Substantial trees shade the front of the house and a pergola is swathed in a wisteria that has engulfed the stone pillars. To one side of the house is a splendid water garden, where a long canal-like pool runs at right angles to the slope, with a shaped pool above it and steps ascending the hill behind. At the foot of the steps a pergola is planted with clematis, roses, and wisteria; at the top, a gravelled cross walk runs across the back of the house, passing under arches of Italian cypress. Exotic flowers and foliage press in all about, giving the impression of a jungle only just kept at bay. But there is much artistry here, with large pots terminating vistas and carefully arranged sitting places. On the eastern side of the garden is the specialist collection of bulbs, with over 200 species. However, the particularly memorable thing about the Clos du Peyronnet is the elegance of Humphrey Waterfield's formal design, blurred by planting of astonishing exuberance, watched over by beautiful old olive trees, gnarled denizens of the past.

Open: By appointment only: individual garden professionals and students of gardening at any reasonable time; groups (minimum 20) also admitted

Further information from:
avenue Aristide Briand,
06500 Menton-Garavan
Tel: 04 93 35 72 15
Fax: 04 93 35 72 25

Nearby sights of interest:
Old town of Menton; La Mortola, Italy (Giardini Hanbury).

Orange *Strelitzia reginae* fringes a pool under an old olive tree.

Château de la Mignarde

Location: 5km (3 miles) NE of Aix-en-Provence by the N96 and the D63

Open: Jun to Aug, daily except Tue, 3–6pm
Open: As above

Further information from:
Les Pinchinats,
13100 Aix-en-Provence
Tel: 04 42 96 41 86

Nearby sights of interest:
Marseille (Basilique de Notre-Dame-de-la-Garde, Vieux Port, Musée Grobet-Labadié, Musée d'Archéologie Méditerranéenne).

Monsieur Mignard was a successful *pâtissier* from the nearby town of Aix-en-Provence, whose son Sauveur improved the family estate in the country, rebuilding the house and laying out a formal garden. He was certainly not ashamed of the source of his family's wealth – cakes adorn the carved stonework that is such an ornament of the garden.

The house is long and low, built of the warm pale apricot-coloured local stone, and the garden has the air of a stage set for some unannounced play, attractive but slightly aimless. In the centre of the deep terrace in front of the house a long rectangular pool is embellished with stone dolphins at either end and a pair of lions spouting water into troughs. At the far end of the terrace, a stone exedra encloses a pool in which Venus looks a little unhappy balanced on the tail of a sea-monster. Above the pool, a white marble Hercules grapples with the Nemean lion. Steps lead down to a lower level, with a pair of whippets on either side, and from here the ground descends gently between groves of plane trees. Statues, scattered more or less regularly on either side of the axis leading away from the house, animate the scene. The vista is closed by an oval pool, beyond which the land falls away. It is said that the statues were part of the original formal garden, executed to the designs of the architect Nicholas Ledoux, but were later rearranged in a less rigid fashion. At all events, the place inspires a mood of melancholy that is far from disagreeable.

Fine statues are disposed in the shade of old plane trees.

Monaco: Jardin Exotique

Location: In Monaco, slightly to the W of the centre

Prince Albert I of Monaco founded the Jardin Exotique in 1914, and endowed it with the plants which he had been collecting since 1899. He chose a dramatic site on a high rocky cliff overlooking the royal palace. The collection is almost exclusively restricted to succulents, of which the garden has one of the largest collections in the world. For the cactus enthusiast the collection will be a revelation, not merely because of the vast number of species, impeccably labelled, but also because of the quality of the individual specimens – several of which are more than a hundred years old, having been acquired as mature specimens by Prince Albert. For the ordinary gardener the place has an almost surrealistic beauty. Paths zigzag down precipitous cliffs through phantasmagoric canyons of cacti, frequently taking the visitor underneath the giant spiny limbs of especially venerable species.

Although the primary function of the garden is that of a botanical collection, it is most attractively laid out with well chosen groups of plants of contrasting colour, foliage, flower, or habit. From the bottom of the garden there are extraordinary views of the plants rearing up on the slopes above. It is beautifully maintained and is especially attractive to visit in winter, when many species are in full flower. Not that flowers are a necessary ornament to some of the more ancient specimens – the elephant-foot tree, *Nolina recurvata*, for example, with gnarled bark resembling the skin of a prehistoric creature.

Open: 15 May to 15 Sep, daily, 9am–7pm; 16 Sep to 14 May, daily, 9am–1pm (closes 19 Nov and 25 Dec)

Further information from:
boulevard du Jardin Exotique,
MC 98002 Monaco Cedex
Tel: 377 93 30 33 65
Fax: 377 93 30 60 74

Nearby sights of interest:
La Mortola, Italy
(Giardino Hanbury).

A chasm of exotic planting, with century-old succulents.

Open: Apr to May, daily,
7am–10pm; Jun to 15 Sep, daily,
7am–11pm; 16 Sep to Oct, daily,
8am–9pm; Nov to Mar, daily,
8am–8pm

Further information from:
quai de la Fontaine, 30000 Nîmes
Tel: 04 66 36 01 36
Fax: 04 66 67 37 25

Nearby sights of interest:
Nîmes (Maison Carrée, Roman
arena); Montpelier (old town,
Musée Fabre); Parc Régional
de Camargue; Pont-du-Gard
(Roman aqueduct).

The nymph of the spring at the
centre of a balustraded island.

9 *Nîmes: Jardin de la Fontaine*

Location: In the centre of town, NW of the Maison Carrée

This is one of the finest of all public gardens in France and unforgettable to anyone who has seen it. Nîmes was a great Roman city and preserves some magnificent buildings from that time: an exquisite temple, the Maison Carrée, and a vast amphitheatre – both dating from around the the first century AD. The garden also has its origins in the Roman period, when the spring here was the site of elaborate baths; the curative properties of its waters were famous throughout the Roman Empire. The existing semi-ruinous Temple of Diana in the garden is probably the remains of a Roman *nymphaeum*. However, the present appearance of the garden goes back to the 1740s, when it was rebuilt by the engineer Jean-Philippe Mareschal. The superb iron railings that encircle the lower part of the garden date from his time. It was he, too, who constructed the long, elegant canal that links the garden so intimately with the city. The centrepiece of the garden is a huge square pool surrounded by balustrades, with a square island at its heart. At each corner *putti* support richly carved giant vases, and in the middle a statue of the nymph of the spring, water pouring from her urn, is accompanied by *putti* gambolling below her seat.

On either side of the pool, groves of limes and planes are embellished with statues and urns. Where the land rises behind the pool, a giant double staircase leads to a balustraded terrace at the foot of a steep wooded hill. This is the Mont Cavalier, the original source of the spring, which was informally landscaped in 1815. Paths lead upwards through woods and at the summit are the remains of the Roman Tour Magne. On the walk back down the hill the Jardin de la Fontaine is gradually revealed through the branches of trees and, from this elevated vantage point, the whole scheme, with its elegant 18th-century logic, is laid out before you. The writer Colette loved the garden: "Elysian refuge . . . . Oh, beautiful garden and beautiful silence, where the only sound is the muted plashing of the green, imperious water, transparent and dark, blue and brilliant as a bright dragon."

Bambouseraie de Prafrance

Location: 13km (8 miles) SW of Alès by the N110 and the D 910

This is dramatic country, with the mountains of the Cévennes rising to the north west. The garden was started in 1850 as a collection of hardy bamboos set in a landscape of primarily – and appropriately – Asiatic trees and shrubs.

The garden commands the interest of gardeners for two reasons. First, it displays almost 200 species and cultivars of bamboo and secondly, parts of the garden, especially jungle areas of giant species, and a distinguished water garden, have remarkable character. This is a full-blown commercial nursery, where bamboos are for sale and may be ordered by mail – some of them giants in 350-litre (77-gallon) containers! Anduze is also a pottery making centre and at Les Enfants de Boisset, which supplied pots to the gardens at Versailles in the 17th century, gardeners may buy the beautiful glazed *pots d'Anduze*.

Open: Mar to Dec, daily, 9.30am to 12 noon, 2–7pm; Jan to Feb, daily except Mon and Tue, 9.30am to 12 noon, 2–7pm

Further information from:
30140 Anduze
Tel: 04 66 61 70 47
or 04 66 61 71 29
Fax: 04 66 61 64 15

Nearby sights of interest:
Potteries of Anduze; Nîmes (Maison Carrée, Roman arena); mountain scenery of the Cévennes.

Jungles of bamboos form colonnades of vegetation.

Villa Ephrussi de Rothschild

Location: 8km (5 miles) E of Nice by the N98

Open: 15 Mar to 1 Nov, daily, 10am–6pm (closes 7pm Jul and Aug); 2 Nov to 14 Feb, Sat, Sun, Public Holidays and school holidays, 10am–6pm, (closes 25 Dec)

Open: As above

Further information from:
avenue E. de Rothschild,
06230 Saint-Jean-Cap-Ferrat
Tel: 04 93 01 45 90
Fax: 04 93 01 31 10

Nearby sights of interest:
Old town of Nice; La Mortola, Italy
(Giardini Hanbury).

The peninsula of St-Jean-Cap-Ferrat, jutting out into the sea beween Nice and Monaco, has long been one of the most favoured sites on the Côte d'Azur. King Leopold II of the Belgians bought land here in 1895 and gradually built up the biggest estate on the peninsula. On his death the villa, Les Cèdres, was sold to Monsieur Marnier-Lapostolle, who created one of the finest botanical gardens on the Côte d'Azur. In 1905, a parcel of land neighbouring the estate, on an even better site, was snapped up under King Leopold's very nose. The buyer was Beatrix de Rothschild, who had been brought up at the Château de Ferrières east of Paris, which had a superb garden designed by Sir Joseph Paxton.

The Spanish garden with brugmansias flanking a canal backed by a classical loggia.

A pavilion in the Florentine garden with modern bush roses.

Beatrix de Rothschild took an
intense interest in the design of
her *palazzino*.

The Temple of Love,
based on the original
at the Petit Trianon
in Versailles.

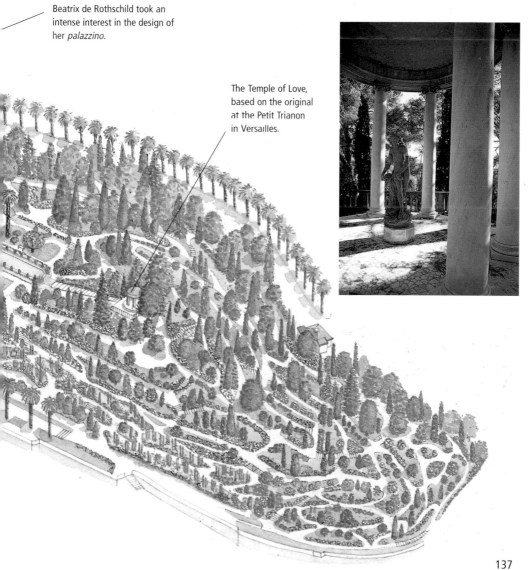

The sunny, southern aspect of the garden has a strongly Mediterranean essence.

The Rothschild land is in a magnificent position, being at the narrowest part of the peninsula on the crest of the spine, with views both west to Villefranche and east to Beaulieu. Here, Beatrix de Rothschild commissioned a luxurious Italianate villa, or palazzino as she liked to call it, involving herself intimately in its design, which was ostensibly carried out by Aaron Messiah, the French partner of the English architect and garden designer Harold Peto. The house took seven years to build and was originally named the Villa Ile de France, after the famous ocean liner on which Beatrix de Rothschild had taken a cruise.

Below the south façade of the house, rocky outcrops were flattened to accommodate a formal layout. An octagonal lily pond lies at the centre of this formal enclosure, now in the heart of the garden, with a canal linked to a cascade emerging from a temple in the form of a rotunda on an eminence on the far side of the garden. The rotunda, with its shallow dome, Corinthian columns, and figure of Venus, was based on the Temple of Love at the Petit Trianon in Versailles (see p.86). The pool and canal establish a strong axis, and around this are arranged lawns, strips of bedding plants, palm trees, and clipped citrus plants. Elsewhere in the garden are individual enclosures with national themes: a Spanish garden with a loggia, canal and splendid brugmansias; an Italian garden with a double sweeping staircase; and a Japanese garden with a glazed pottery temple. Everywhere there are wonderful views over the sea.

A visit to the villa itself is essential. The interior is light and airy, exquisitely furnished in the grandest 18th-century French taste, with paintings and ornaments to match. The views of the garden from the windows of the villa show how strongly the two are related. The whole place, magnificently maintained, is a triumphant and irresistible expression of *le goût Rothschild*. "The mixture is lighthearted – puff pastry" as Beatrix's English cousin, Miriam Rothschild, accurately described it.

The elegant pink walls of the villa contrast coolly with the exotic trees and plants before them.

Opposite page:
The rocky slopes of the *cap*, with views of the Mediterranean.

Villa Thuret

Location: Between Cannes and Nice, on the Cap d'Antibes

 Open: All year, daily except Sat, Sun and Public Holidays, 8am–5.30pm

Further information from:
62, boulevard du Cap,
06606 Antibes
Tel: 04 93 67 88 66
Fax: 04 93 67 88 25

Nearby sights of interest:
Old town of Nice.

Gustave Thuret, botanist and expert on seaweeds, lived here, and over a period of twenty years he amassed a great collection of rare plants – among them the first eucalyptus to be planted on the Côte d'Azur. The interest of the place to gardeners is the great collection of tender woody plants – no less than 3,000 species – which are grown here. The garden specializes in certain groups of plants: Australian genera of the myrtle family, the cycad family, and the Proteaceae show some of the most exotic species. Other collections are less showy, such as a complete collection of every species of cypress. In four hectares of exotic jungle the visitor may wander at will studying plants rarely seen in any other European collection and inhaling the delicious scents of eucalyptus.

 # *Villa Val Rahmeh*

Location: Above the port of Menton-Garavan

Open: May to Sep, daily, 10am–12.30pm; Oct to Apr, daily, 10am–12.30pm, 2–5pm

Further information from:
avenue Saint-Jacques,
06500 Menton
Tel: 04 93 35 86 72
Fax: 04 93 28 89 75

Nearby sights of interest:
La Mortola, Italy
(Giardini Hanbury).

The Italianate parterre with roses, santolina and Anduze pots.

The owner of this estate is now the Muséum d'Histoire Naturelle so that it is, in effect, the Mediterranean outpost of the Jardin des Plantes in Paris. This is misleading, for its most attractive quality is that of a rather secretive private garden of luxuriant planting rather than that of a scientific institution. It is, in fact, an English garden in this most English part of the Côte d'Azur, made by a retired Governor of Malta, General Sir Percy Radcliffe, who built the house in 1925 and started to make a garden. On Radcliffe's death it was taken over by Dr Campbell, physician to the English community in Menton. His daughter, Maybud, inherited it and it is chiefly to her passion for plants that we owe the interest of the place today.

The garden has a precipitous site on the slopes above the port of Menton-Garavan. A curving drive leads up to the house, lined with an avenue of palms (*Phoenix canariensis*), underplanted with the tender Mexican sage *Salvia guaranitica*. In front of the house a balustraded terrace has spectacular views to the sea, and is laid out with a parterre-like formal garden with paths of brick and gravel, and a pattern of box-edged beds and clumps of bird of paradise plant (*Strelitzia reginae*) and kangaroo apple (*Solanum aviculare*). This is the only formal part of the garden, which elsewhere consists of narrow paths threading their way among groves of exotic plants. The garden is well cared for and it is to be hoped that now, in institutional ownership, it will manage to preserve that precious character, so attractive to visitors, of a private domain.

Glossary

allée (French) Pathway which is bordered on either side with plants, either trees or hedges.

Arts and Crafts A group of artists and craftsmen – including John Ruskin and William Morris – who influenced English garden designers such as Gertrude Jekyll. They used local building materials and traditional plants, rejecting the regimented artificiality of Victorian planting.

bassin (French) A small formal pool which is usually made of stone.

belvedere (Italian) Ornamental building that commands an extensive view.

berceau (French) A shaded arbour, often with seating, which is enclosed with plants.

bosquet (French) A formal grove, often with a decorative glade, in which statues or other ornaments may be placed.

buffet d'eau (French) A type of fountain, popular in 17th-century France, in the form of steps over which the water falls.

Chinoiserie (French) A Chinese fashion in the decorative arts, especially popular in England and Germany in the 18th century, fostered by trading contacts with the Far East.

cour d'honeur (French) The principal courtyard of a great house.

exedra (Greek) An ornamental, open garden building which is often curved with a bench inside.

jardin à l'anglaise (French) An informal garden arrangement of shrubs, lawns, and trees which was popular in England in the 18th century. Literally "Garden in the English style".

miroir d'eau (French) A large formal pool which is designed in such a way that it is reflective, usually of the château.

mosaïculture (French) A method of planting which dates from 17th-century France which mixes carpet bedding with annuals in a tightly ordered pattern.

parterre (French) A formal bedding with low hedges, often of box, disposed in a regular way and often incorporating topiary, urns, or other decorative devices.

parterre de broderie (French) A particular form of parterre in which the shapes of the hedges are arranged in long flowing patterns which imitate embroidery.

potager (French) Kitchen garden, usually formal or decorative.

Biographies

André, Edouard François (1840–1911) French landscape architect who designed a number of gardens throughout Europe.

Blaikie, Thomas (1758–1838) Scottish designer who introduced English landcape style to Parc Monceau and Bagatelle.

Desgots, Claude (d1732) French garden designer, from a long line of royal gardeners, who also worked in England and Germany.

Duchêne, Achille (1866–1947) French garden designer who restored gardens at Vaux-le-Vicomte and Courances, as well as working in Germany and England.

Evelyn, John (1620–1706) English diarist who improved horticulture and introduced exotic species to England.

La Quintinye, Jean Baptiste de (1624–68) Louis XIV's gardener, who designed the kitchen garden at Versailles.

Lemercier, Jacques (c1585–1654) French architect who designed parts of the Louvre and Sorbonne and many other buildings.

Le Nôtre, André (1613–1700) French landscape architect, one of the most important of the Baroque period, who laid out gardens at Vaux-le-Vicomte and Versailles.

Index

Acknowledgements

I received much help from garden owners all over France – I am most grateful to them all. Many kind friends made suggestions of places to visit which were immensely helpful. At my publisher I have very much appreciated the advice, help and friendliness of Jane Aspden, Guy Croton, Michèle Byam, Selina Mumford, and Anna Nicholas. My wife, Caroline, has been a marvellous help in every way, as always.

Patrick Taylor, *September 1997*

Photographic Acknowledgements

Front jacket: Hugh Palmer
Back jacket: Mise au Point br; Patrick Taylor cr, tr; Caroline Taylor back flap

t=top; b=bottom; c=centre; r=right; l=left

EXPLORER /A. Philippon 140. Garden Picture Library /Erika Craddock 2/3, 33b, /Nigel Temple 74. Garden Matters 138t. Robert Harding Picture Library /Explorer 128, /JACOBS 49, /Roy Rainford 67, /Nedra Westwater 84. Lamontagne 26, 34. Mise au Point 36, /Yann Monel 94. Hugh Palmer 12, 14/15, 46t, 61tr, 121. Annette Schreiner 87. Scope /Jean-Luc Barde 22, 135, /Jacques Guillard 41, 60/61t, 63t, 65, 81tl, 137b, /Michel Guillard 53, 85, /Noel Hautemaniere 101, /Laurent Juvigny 95, /Daniele Taulin-Hommell 81tr, /Guy Thouvenin 137t, /VMF/GALERON 7 17. Sygma /M. Pelletier 60b, 62.
Patrick Taylor 5, 7, 8t, 9t, 9b, 10/11, 13, 16, 17, 18, 19, 20, 21, 23, 24, 25, 27, 28, 29, 30, 31, 32, 33t, 35, 37, 38, 39, 40, 42, 43, 44, 45, 46b, 47, 48, 51, 54, 55, 56, 57, 58, 59, 61b, 63b, 64, 66, 68, 69, 70, 71, 72, 73, 74, 75, 76, 77, 78, 79, 80, 81b, 82, 83, 86, 89, 90/91, 92, 93, 96, 97, 98, 99, 100, 103, 104/105, 106, 107, 108, 109, 110, 111, 112, 113, 114, 115, 116, 117, 118, 119, 120, 122, 123, 125, 126/127, 129, 130, 131, 132, 133, 134, 136, 138b, 139